At Home with Designers and Tastemakers

At Home with Designers and Tastemakers

Creating Beautiful and Personal Interiors

by Susanna Salk and Stacey Bewkes

CREATORS OF THE *QUINTESSENCE AT HOME WITH* VIDEO SERIES

Rizzoli
NEW YORK

New York · Paris · London · Milan

Table of Contents

··•●•··

Introduction
Susanna Salk

··•●•··

I had only met Stacey for a couple of minutes when I had the idea for our video series and wanted her to be my partner in it. I literally signed a book for her at a local store (where we were introduced), and then as I drove home, the concept of filming designers in their own homes downloaded itself into my brain.

Of course, I already followed Stacey's much revered blog, *Quintessence*, and I knew how respected she was by the design community, as by me. And I could see that she knew how to work in Final Cut Pro, as she had posted a video story capturing my former editor at *House & Garden* at her home in Rhode Island. Between the two of us, we already knew many of the top interior designers around the world, from shoots, dinner parties, and events. "We know how smart and fearless and fun they are, but so many only see their work, and that's not enough," I told her, as I crossed my own threshold.

"Two-dimensional shots of their work in magazines only can offer so much. Let's break the barrier," she added excitedly.

"Let's open their world up and give design a voice," I added, knowing we both didn't have to say anything more. We were all in, even if we didn't know the town where the other lived. Our shared intent was enough.

We quickly made a list of our Top 10 asks: Some were already friends, while others were admittedly reaches. We divided the list between us, and within an hour we were already texting—the first of thousands to each other—that everyone had said yes.

And so it began, filming at first in our hometowns in Connecticut, New York, and Nantucket. But as the views and subscribers increased, so did the distance we traveled from them: to Tangier, Cartagena, and Paris. And our support rippled back. We walked down a street in Charleston, and a woman told us how much she loved the series. I sat next to a priest on an airplane on the way to Rome who recognized me. We had comments from places as far away as Poland and Brazil telling us how these videos mattered in their lives. We celebrated ten thousand overall views and then one hundred thousand. Then a million monthly views.

The designers themselves began approaching us, telling us how they loved how we revealed their silverware drawers, clothing closets, gardens, and paint color mistakes. There was no page count that could cap the tours, as is the case with magazines: we could make the videos any length we wanted, and our biggest criticism was that people wanted them longer. We did our own marketing, editing, social media, driving, and travel arrangements. We shoved Power Bars into our mouths while inputting the next destination into our GPS. I always drove, and Stacey navigated. We quizzed our children about their homework along the way and obsessed about the next houses we wanted to visit when we saw something delectable posted on Instagram.

We never turned the radio on or ever ran out of things to tell each other. We often said, "Oh . . . my . . . god . . . " in exact unison as we drove up yet another spectacular driveway.

Along the way, we learned about audio (still a challenge), that I have to remember to brush the back of my hair, and to always get extra B-roll of any dogs in the house. (Interestingly, we never met any cats.) This kind of learning curve one expects.

I'm always preaching to others the idea of borrowing when it comes to design because it's never a direct

translation. If you love the salmon color that Timothy Corrigan painted the dining room in his chateau in France, try it in the guest bathroom of your Chicago apartment. If Bunny Williams's custom terrazzo tile floor in her Manhattan kitchen dazzles you but is beyond your budget, consider stenciling your own design to bring yours to life. Obsessed by how Alexa Hampton creates visual landscapes via her collections of classical treasures, but you're not a seasoned collector or, in fact, you don't collect anything yet? Buy three of something you love. There, you've started collecting just the way she did.

What I didn't expect was the infectious power of the designers' homes upon my own little one. No matter how far we traveled and how long it took to get home, I'd always cross my own threshold elated. My inspiration cup was full, and I somehow had to pour it into my own rooms. And I did. For example, I came back after shooting in some of the grandest English country houses and bought a porcelain vase at a local consignment shop for twenty-five bucks. I would have walked right by it before. I loved how Johnson Hartig cheekily pinned his own luxurious Schumacher wallpaper trompe l'oeil pattern of blue-and-white platters behind his stove so much that I immediately ordered a yard and then cut and arranged it myself as soon as I got home,

complete with thumbtacks. That visual gratification always makes the leap for me. If I have an emotional response seeing other people live with something I love, then why not treat myself to seeing something similar every day? And the chain of inspiration is infinite: Once I painted my library bookshelves a glossy aubergine after being inspired by a similar hue in Katie Ridder and Peter Pennoyer's dining room. A friend came over and scoped the idea for the shelves in her son's nursery. And then another mutual friend chose it for her front door.

This book is like a personal photo album and somewhat of a reverse course from the video series: We took some of our favorite visits over the years and distilled them into images, giving them their own chapter and adding our memories.

Over seven years, one hundred video visits would seem plentiful, but the journey never gets old or jaded. People making their lives more beautiful and functional and emotionally fulfilling through the design of personal touches is the greatest gift we can give ourselves and our families and friends. We don't have to be experts; we just need to allow ourselves to listen to them. The point has always been to give design a voice. May you find your design voice along the way as I have.

PAGE 6: I love to bring both real and imagined nature into my rooms whenever possible. And nothing brings me more pleasure than creating visual landscapes. Here in the sun porch as you enter my house, examples from designers' homes over the years have shown me the power of combining different heights, textures, colors and mediums not just across the surface but above and below it.

PAGE 8: This is my mud room, but that didn't stop me from making it whimsical and bold. I wanted my visitors to feel like they were falling down a rabbit hole as they stepped inside my little creative world. Why should we skimp on putting some of our favorite art work and colors in a space that is, perhaps, most used in the entire house?

PAGE 9, CLOCKWISE FROM TOP LEFT: I display my jewelry flat across John Derian trays and inside vintage bowls. I never store anything away. I believe that you should always see and use everything you have. If you don't have room for it, or if you haven't worn it in a year, you should give it away to someone who might.

Johnson Hartig's ingenious placement of his amazing Plates and Platters wallpaper for Schumacher behind his stove as a kind of backsplash inspired me to order it as soon as I came back from shooting in his fabulous Los Angeles home. He used pins to tack it up simply, with an elegant insouciance that I copied for my immediate gratification. There's no need to always take our design choices so seriously!

My son Winston's bedroom makes me happy every time I walk past it, even when he's not there. It reminds that, no matter how small, every space should be packed with the personality of those who live there.

I wanted my television room to feel like a jewel box. I don't watch TV much but there was no way that I was going to let it feel like a neglected pass-through space, Once I found just the right blue (this color inspired after we filmed at Miles Redd's extraordinary townhouse)

I layered in yellow velvet curtains and a beautiful chinoiserie rug I spied forgotten in a consignment store for two hundred dollars.

Leopard velvet cushions always make a sofa chicer. These are from Etsy and for a song despite the fact they lend a rich feeling to the green velvet sofa from Article.

I was intent on painting my fireplace black. And Amanda Brook's use of a gold mirror above her living room fireplace was direct inspiration. I'm always leaning on the visual validation of rooms I love to help inform the choices in my own. Soon after I published a picture of this on instagram, a follower said my living room helped inform her choices. So it keeps getting paid forward!

OPPOSITE, TOP: My barn is over two hundred years old and used to be the social gathering spot for visitors from all the inns around Lake Waramaug. It was filled with junk when I purchased the property and now houses year-round gatherings of my beloved friends and family. The bookcase was saved and I keep many of the dusty old novels found within its shelves along with some of my favorite books. My boys' musical equipment awaits their return from whenever they visit from the West Coast. The painting was done by an artist whose sculpture I admired from the side of the road whenever I drove by. I love the combination of hanging modern art against the old beams and walls.

OPPOSITE, BOTTOM: I found the barn's original simple bar and moved it under a giant mirror I discovered down in the basement. From here I can serve my guests drinks and watch ensuing ping pong matches.

ABOVE: Putting in a pool was my biggest luxury and one I do not take lightly! I use it several times a day from May through September and delight (along with my three dogs) not only its saline waters but its view of the barn and the surrounding nature.

At Home with

Jill Sharp Weeks

...●●●...

My infatuation with A.T.J. (aka "All Things Jill") started when our paths briefly crossed in Atlanta years ago on a job for Ballard Designs, where she was creative director and I was styling for one of their catalog shoots. I instantly wanted to emulate her artistic yet gamine style, from her shearling clogs (which I bought via my phone while literally standing in front of her) to her pixielike haircut, which, lucky for me, I realized I could not pull off. Jill, in turn, bought the Comme des Garçons T-shirt I was wearing on her phone, and then we talked about our love of dogs and decor. As soon as I returned to Connecticut, my rescue puppy chewed the newly arrived clogs, a detail she adored as soon as I relayed it.

Cut to almost ten years later: I am in Charleston for a book signing, strolling past its iconic historic homes, when I stop in front of one in particular—its traditional eighteenth-century brick facade had been wedded to a sleek, beguiling modern addition, punctuated by a massive outdoor lantern and three forty-foot-tall sycamore trees pollarded to create sculptural, chic green lollipops. It's all so unexpected yet completely appropriate, respecting its surroundings while raising the bar to whatever can be imagined. "I want to meet whoever would do this," I think. Later, while signing books, I hear that it is Jill Sharp Weeks who lives behind that beacon of fabulousness. "Of course, who else?!" I think.

A few years later, when I finally get to go inside the 1790 house to capture her life there for the video series, I learn that the large L-shaped addition used to be a parking lot. Now it houses the Weeks' sublime kitchen, pantry, fireplace sitting area, powder room, and guest bedroom spaces. Jill walks down the staircase of the now-soaring two-story space to greet us wearing a boldly striped ticking cotton caftan. "I live for a good stripe, both on my body and in rooms and gardens," she says. Around her neck is her signature layering of three necklaces: some shells from Papua New Guinea, a custom-made piece by her nieces, and an oversized African tribal adornment. Everything in Jill's world is a kind of talisman, and the vibe is palpable.

Growing up surrounded by her great-great-uncle's paintings (American impressionist William S. Robinson), an intensely creative mother with a penchant for throwing wild dinner parties, a father (chemical engineer) with a strong passion for photography and a stint living in Japan as a teenager, Jill's unique styling is obviously rooted firmly in her DNA. But it's how utterly personally she expresses it, taking every detail a step further without being fussy, that resonates—the way dozens of potted myrtle plants populate the counter in the outdoor bar, which is lined in shimmering tile handmade in Morocco; the way former Dyptique candle holders now contain vintage hotel silverware Jill collects and then monograms with numbers to delight dinner guests; the way a rock from Maine coexists on a Belgian bureau next to a bowl of Ray and Jill's wedding matches, their backs inscribed with the following mantras: WE LOVE: CLEVER WORDSMITHS, FORAGERS, BEAUTIFUL PROBLEM SOLVERS, CARING URBANISTS, ARCHITECTURE FREAKS, DOG LOVERS + PEOPLE HELPING PEOPLE, GET YOUR VEG ON GET YOUR LOVE ON.

We sit down in the Eames molded shell chairs for a lunch of local lettuce and fresh fish, with mango, mint, and lime zest. I ask Jill what the material is on the addition's facade. "It's new brick hand-applied with brick slurry, which is crushed oyster shells, lime, and a little magic," she says. Only in Jill's world does brick coating sound like an elixir, yummy enough to drink.

Later, when we ride bikes through the city's cobblestone streets, she tells me about her and Ray's upcoming trip to Scotland and how they already have bought plaid waistcoats and tartan patchwork kilts. I want to travel with them, to see the world through their wide-open eyes and to see what they bring home to Charleston.

When we return, Jill has transformed the entry hall into a huge dinner party setting using tables she stores in the basement for just such moments and has draped them with oversize gray Spanish truck tarps. Suspended from the ceiling are straw animal heads, which set the stage for the Picasso and his Muses party Jill is generously hosting in honor of our coming to town. It turns out Jill and I have both chosen Françoise Gilot as our character muse. I've counted on a simple black wig for my transformation, but Jill wears a minimalist vintage cotton dress with a black wooden bull napkin ring now converted into a chic choker—an homage to Picasso's love of forceful creatures. A crown of ivy is woven through her hair. "I think I was a weaver in another life," she says with a smile.

On our final day, we take the Weeks' New England–style boat, the *October* (named after their "love month," which holds both their anniversary and birthdays), for a gentle cruise out into Charleston's bay. Custom-fit from aft to stern, it touts gray-stained teak with black-, white-, and putty-striped upholstery and zebra-hide pillows. Even the towels have been embroidered with the Weeks' logo, an octopus holding an anchor.

Jill has prepared a luscious charcuterie board along with homemade gazpacho served in individual jam jars. Later, as I watch Ray lazily steer us homeward, Jill dashes below deck to grab us some blankets. Pure happiness is spread across Ray's face, and I understand why he is so excited to be heading home.

··•●•··

PREVIOUS SPREAD: "There's nothing like creating a sublime material language in a room," says Jill, and here she's combined the rough-textured Belgian bluestone floors and counter with American white oak cabinets and miles of Moroccan *zellige* wall tiles and Swedish and French cutting boards. "And I love using drawers in my kitchen designs. It's not only easier to see everything, but I also like the linear lines." The abstract painting is by William McLure.

OPPOSITE, TOP LEFT: Jill and I taking a pause from biking throughout Charleston. "It's the patina of the city—the faded color and textures of its over three-hundred-year-old history—that influences me most," says Jill. "And it's had a huge impact on the way I designed and layered our home."

OPPOSITE, TOP RIGHT: "When it came to creating the addition to our 1790 home, the goal was for it to feel like something that could have been there but that had been updated at some time," says Jill. The steel windows and overly large lantern are a trademark of her projects. "One of the things I most love about this new cream brick and slurry facade is how diminutive it feels next to the house that sits to the left. It is both bold and humble."

OPPOSITE, RIGHT MIDDLE: "I live for a good, clever still life," says Jill. Here, a glossy-white painted African stool supports a candle with a modern-primitive doodle and a framed Picasso lithograph. Jill and Ray still use and cherish the matchbooks Jill designed and had custom-printed to celebrate their coupling in 2015.

OPPOSITE, RIGHT BOTTOM: One of Ray's many passions is boating, and the couple spends tons of time on the water with friends exploring Charleston and the surrounding shorelines.

OPPOSITE, BOTTOM: In the back garden, live myrtle topiaries are piled high with key limes and black beans covering the soil. This folly serves as a bartending station when Jill and Ray throw big parties. "Off go the plants and out comes the liquor!" says Jill.

PREVIOUS SPREAD: "Adding all this wide-open, bright natural daylight as an addition to the old home we purchased made it feel so fresh," says Jill. "This space is huge and gets pushed around depending on what needs to happen." Behind the hand-blown mirrored panel, done by the maestro of mirror in Charleston, Bob Hines, is the pantry. "Bob's process of creating this mirror is a dying art, and I value every piece of his that we have. The wall that faces the kitchen is open glass to expose our provisions and dishes."

OPPOSITE: "This is the first island I have ever done, and it made me so nervous," says Jill. "I like flexibility in rooms, kitchens included, so this was a real brain teaser. I ended up taking apart what had been a really long table and using it as the island counter. Local blacksmith Sean Ahern made the steel posts and straps and forged our initials and wedding date into the steel." The zebra-hide placemats are well-worn stool seats to vintage tripod stools. "Thinking out of the box is my normal resting state," says Jill.

"One of my complete happy places that always makes me smile," says Jill of her pantry. Some things here she has had for forty years and styled in many national ad campaigns as props. "I adore a utilitarian aesthetic and always am looking for things with numbers, letters, and handles, and a heft of another time. I also always look for small dishes and repurposed containers to add height and spontaneity to our tables. I never do the same thing twice."

"I had always thought throwing a Picasso and his Muses party would be fun, but this seated supper, held in our entry hall using tables stored in our Downton Abbey-esque basement, exceeded my expectations," says Jill of the party she kindly threw Stacey and me when we came to shoot.

"With his Spanish roots, I played into Picasso's love of bulls by hanging straw donkey and bull heads from the hallway above. And from his art, I borrowed the color palette and roughness by using a Spanish truck tarp that is patched and marred and imperfectly perfect like his paintings as the tablecloth." The finishing touch was hay stuffed into leather horses and name-tag holders. "It is this level of personal expression when I am at my most content," says Jill.

"I don't do pretty. I do strong, edited, masculine spaces. I adore tension in rooms," says Jill. This wall of art from the 1950s was hung without a plan. The brutalist console is new but works because of the provenance of the art. The stairs lead to the attic Pilates studio.

This room, to the right of the steel entry door, was designed to just look chic but not give its function away: It has a Murphy bed that folds down and turns into the coolest of guest rooms. "It was designed with the precision of campaign-style furniture and is like an opening into another era."

ABOVE: "The day that the 8'9" solid slab bluestone master trough sink arrived, I knew that I was married to the most understanding partner in crime," says Jill. "My husband, Ray Weeks, ended up finishing building this house, and it occurred while I was recovering from my second cancer. I sat there and dreamt things up, and he and our architect Peter Block made it come to life. The house will always hold this overwhelming feeling for me. Pure true love with no boundaries."

OPPOSITE: In the main bedroom, the plaster lamps are some of the most special things Jill and Ray own—from a favorite Houston dealer. The duvet was made by sewing together flat sheets. The sculpture on the rear wall is two sheets of French plywood used to cut marble and stone countertops on. "It is total art to me," says Jill. "But the best part of this bedroom is that there is a TV mounted flush into the wall to the right that pushes out with a button to be about five inches in front of our faces."

At Home with

•••●•••

Lulu
Powers

•••●•••

Who doesn't want to visit someone named Lulu? "It's like her last name fuels the cuteness even more," I tell Stacey, as we walk up to the gate of Lulu's hidden 1927 bungalow in West Hollywood. A sign on the very unimposing gate says *Chien Lunatique*. It is quiet except for the tinkling of a nearby water fountain and the lush tree branches and flowering bougainvillea moving against one another in the warm California breeze. No sign of Lulu or said *chien*.

We already feel at home, so we enter into the oasis as three very sane and sassy Bichons come bounding over to greet us. As we learn their names through their ID tags—Mister Pickles, Teddy Kennedy, and Sparky—Lulu calls us.

"I completely forgot you were coming, but I am so excited you are here!" she says in her wonderfully free-spirited voice. "I am wrapping up a catering job. Pour yourself a Sneeky. There's something delish in the pitcher!" Lulu aptly calls herself an "entertainologist," and "Sneeky" is her catchphrase for something yummy (and maybe slightly naughty) to sip.

Even though she says she will be there in fifteen minutes, we know that in L.A. this is impossible, so we make a dash outdoors to the "Sneek Easy," a bar that feels more like a workshop meets lab meets hot gossip and rendezvous spot rather than just a place to refresh oneself. It's articulated with blue-and-white tile, a copper-and-wood bar (inspired by the one at Il Buco in Manhattan), and an enormous white stone sink surrounded by bowls of blood oranges, buckets of sunflowers, silver-and-brass candlesticks, and even a ship's lantern. (There's even a neon Sneek Easy sign her husband, Steve, gifted her hanging in the outdoor bar.) The vibe is as distinct as her signature ice cubes, which are filled with fresh flowers and fruits, and every drawer reveals the perfect tool to concoct something creative, from juicers to jiggers.

We pour ourselves a kumquat margarita from a waiting pitcher (made from fresh kumquats from the yard), then we wait in her backyard pavilion, which every East Coaster dreams about (and Lulu gets this hailing from Connecticut herself) in February: a chocolate-brown-striped tented canopy with green furniture that seamlessly blends with all the verdant foliage. We sip our drinks to the sound of the nearby fountain, and our jet lag melts away.

When Lulu does arrive—her über blonde hair wrapped fetchingly, layered with delicious chunky jewelry, and sporting sunglasses you immediately want to own—she sweeps you up in an exuberance that makes you feel like you've known her all your life. Her home's interior makes you feel similarly special—the living room walls are painted a distinctly bright blue, like skies you'd be lucky to experience no matter which coast you live on. In corners there are stacks of books you know she's read, next to plants and treasures of wonderfully mysterious provenance, including an indoor bar tray with mismatched glassware beside an antique bust that is topped with a hat belonging to Lulu's late father. Keep in mind this is a woman who created a backgammon table for her husband that switches into a desk with just a flip of its surface and lined the board's sides with candies in glass jars.

Wallpaper is big here ("I think it makes a room sing," explains Lulu), from the soft, silvery glean of the wallpapered entry with its wandering vines of soft lilac and chocolate that envelop you, or the splashy blue-and-white palm print in the breakfast nook, to the more sedate blue-and-yellow toile in the guest bedroom, topped by an antique portrait found in Seattle for $125. "My house evolved naturally," says Lulu with a smile. "I guess I'm just a chic hoarder."

After our filming is done, we go to repose in the front garden, where birds cluster happily on a fountain's rippled surface. Palm fronds tickle the tops of my head as we sit on wrought-iron furniture canopied by luscious palm trees. It's a secluded, meditative space right outside Lulu's front gate. "My dad used to come in from his big vegetable garden in Connecticut where I grew up and say, 'I am going to have myself a little Sneeky,'" Lulu reminisces, rightly anticipating I would ask her to tell me this story. "He would then get his little drink in a beautiful glass—he always hated plastic—and he would sit in this chair that was next to his garden, sip, and watch his garden grow." We toast to a day wonderfully spent and then do the same.

··•●•··

PREVIOUS SPREAD: "We fell in love with this bust at a store called Pickets, in Fairfield, Connecticut," says Lulu. "As soon as we got it home, I knew I was going to make him an ode to my father. I change his hats, glasses, and scarves whenever the mood strikes. This green one was really my dad's, which he wore often. It makes me happy."

OPPOSITE, TOP: Lulu and I pose in what Lulu calls her "salon." Her husband, Stevie, got the mirror at Brenda Antin before they were married, and it now rests on a ten-dollar bench covered with Scalamandré fabric. "We are in here mostly at night with a fire roaring," says Lulu. "It's a magical room with romantic, subtle light and lots of candles! If you lose your keys in this light you'll never find them."

OPPOSITE, BOTTOM: The salon is a feast for the eyes with what Lulu calls "lots of scapes." Layering is her passion. "The biggest compliment was when my friend, designer Mary McDonald, said to me, 'People pay big money to get this look, and it just comes naturally to you.'" The black Scalamandré vases are a favorite of Lulu's: "They are statement pieces in themselves, and you don't even need the flowers in them."

PREVIOUS SPREAD: The backgammon board, in orange, brown, and champagne suede with dark wood, can flip and become a table. Another backgammon board sits below the big table just in case Lulu and Stevie have more takers. "I love the orange chairs," she says. "When I found them at a pop-up shop, I knew exactly where they were meant to go."

OPPOSITE: This is a painting of Stevie's Uncle John. "We found it under the bed in the guest room at his grandmother's house and asked if we could have it," says Lulu.

FOLLOWING SPREAD: In Lulu's backyard, the cabana makes for a great outdoor room. Pops of color, plants, and lots of pillows are always present.

ABOVE: Lulu's outdoor laboratory, where she creates everything from flower arrangements to painting (she keeps her tools in big Ball jars) to writing. The wooden bowl—always filled with lemons and limes—is one hundred years old.

OPPOSITE: The heart of Lulu and Stevie's home: The Sneek Easy, an outdoor bar that's a feast for the eyes. One of her signature favorite "Sneekys" (cocktail) or "Strokeys" (nonalcoholic) is an orange Tangerine Sneeky adorned with a rose petal ice cube. There's also a smattering of her favorite ice buckets here and a sign reminding us that every day is special: "It's always someone's birthday, so why not celebrate?" says Lulu.

"The best room in our house is our nook," says Lulu. "We love to 'fellowship' here, meaning to gather with friends or family for coffee or a chat. . . . I love this wallpaper, called Palmeral, by House of Hackney. It's just happy. My kitchen is blue, the palms are blue, and my outdoor bar is blue, like the sea, always calming. And this happens to be the dogs' favorite room: they watch me cook nearby in the kitchen while sitting on the chairs and ottoman."

Stevie's office is the ultimate man cave, holding all his collections of vintage photography books, fashion magazines, little lamps, trophies, keepsakes, and vintage cameras throughout the shelves. "I like the way he made the covers of the books face out," says Lulu. "It's almost like a portrait wall. You could spend all day in there just looking at the books or daydreaming. Some days I just go in there to take a nap while he's working. I find it calming."

"This Pierre Deux wallpaper has been up for twenty-one years and reminds me of my beloved East Coast upbringing," says Lulu. Old fire hoses made into lamps were found at John Rugge, an antiques store in Nantucket.

At Home with

•••●•••

Suzanne Rheinstein

•••●•••

While filming Suzanne Rheinstein at her home in Hancock Park, she told us she had bought a weekend retreat in Montecito, sight unseen, from her hospital bed during a recovery from a bone-shattering accident in South Africa that required multiple surgeries. It was a decision that felt both timely and spontaneous, and gave her a unique opportunity to spread and point her design wings in a different, yet equally elegant and personal, direction.

"My house in Los Angeles is a scrapbook of our family life, which I cherish. Here, my rooms are filled with art and objects with a certain lightness that I love in my Montecito getaway," she explains moments after our arrival, while handing us sparkling white tea with ginger and cranberry in glasses I instantly covet. Everything here, nestled in the foothills of the Santa Ynez mountains, reflects Suzanne's commitment to her location, literally top to bottom. "There is a certain blue-green that is often used on traditional Santa Barbara windows, and I used my version of it to paint my front door. These doors were inspired by ones I saw in Mallorca, a place that inspired many details of the house and garden. The colors are subdued and subtle, and take their cues from the light that pours in from the mountain and sea. The plaster, both inside and out, is integrally colored the same shade of off-white. The shapes of the rooms shine as the outside shines."

The roof was her finishing touch (and, oh, how we obsessed!), with the old asphalt tiles coming off and replaced by flat terracotta tiles made by an American vendor. "Getting the right mix of brown and red was time-consuming but worth it," she adds. "And then they were all rubbed with sand to get a mellow look."

Inside her getaway, the hand-plastered walls play a bucolic role in showing off the simple yet detailed lines of the custom hardware, made in Belgium. They also set the stage for all the artwork Suzanne has cherry-picked to bring joy to her days. "From the beginning, I wanted to fill the house with works on paper. I love drawings, old and contemporary, as they have an immediacy, and the hand of the artists is so evident," she explains, while pointing out Picasso drawings from Antibes in 1946 that the artist had reproduced as pochoirs and that are now draped around the living room fireplace and adjacent wall. "I love looking at the lines, as lines."

Despite the serious provenance of so many of the pieces here, there's nothing formal about this place. There isn't even a dining room, and we take our lunch break on the Sawkill table in the kitchen, sitting on slipcovered chairs with wheels that her granddaughters love scooting across the Echelle-patterned, wide-plank, white oak floors. "I knew I didn't want a formal dining room in this house," says Suzanne, serving us Persian barley salad with mint, citrus, and freshly caught Santa Barbara spot prawns. "The weather in Santa Barbara is too delightful not to eat outdoors picnic-style whenever possible, and when we are inside, I want to keep it simple."

After McConnell's Turkish coffee ice cream, a local favorite, we head back to capture more shots. I can't help but notice the abundance of books and places to read them everywhere, especially the designated Reading Room, with

its elongated chaise complete with Princess and the Pea-stacked mattresses (covered in Suzanne's own Indian Zag pattern for Lee Jofa fabric) outstretched next to the house's original 1970s fireplace. Hanging behind it are two-hundred-year-old faded blue-and-white plates rescued from a shipwreck, still with encrustations on them. It's the perfect setting to dream and read about faraway places. "I've filled the shelves with what I call the essential books—on gardens and art—with inspiring pictures here," she says. "And I keep my books of fiction and highfalutin' ideas in my bedroom."

After lunch, we stroll and chat through her lavender pathways and hedges of rosemary with bees happily buzzing beside us like eager listeners. We eventually go back into the house, into the flower room, with its practical zinc countertops. Here, Suzanne's beloved tools are always ready for her next inspiration: clippers, baskets, jute twine, and too many hats and containers to count. "My favorite flowers aren't flowers at all, but often leaves from the metrosideros trees, as I love their silvery color, and when they bloom, their red starry flowers attract the soft hum of bees," says Suzanne.

As we finish the day filming in her main bedroom, I can't help but linger at the garden views outside the bedroom's floor-to-ceiling windows with French doors, and she instantly understands. "I love waking up and being surrounded by a garden on three sides of me," she says. "And reading the paper in here over toast, café au lait, and local tangerines is heaven."

But the best day begins and ends with family. "I love welcoming my daughter and her young girls here from the East Coast," says Suzanne. "We do s'mores in the fireplace and draw in the garden, and then snuggle on the mattress and read. I built this house for exactly that."

··●●··

PREVIOUS SPREAD: "I wanted a slightly rustic flower room," says Suzanne. "Totes, twine, clippers, and sun hats—all ready for going to the farmers market or for gardening. Right outside is my old continental potting table."

OPPOSITE, TOP AND BOTTOM RIGHT: The pergola is a favorite place of Suzanne's—the dappled sunlight through the bamboo and honeysuckle vine has a sweet fragrance. From the comfortable banquette one can see the Santa Ynez Mountains. "The sky goes on forever," says Suzanne. "And I love to enjoy a fire on a cool Santa Barbara evening."

OPPOSITE, BOTTOM LEFT: Spears share space with a beautiful 1960s graphite drawing by Jay Rivkin.

ABOVE: An old Belgian flower-arranging table Suzanne uses for potting.

OPPOSITE: "The tapis vert is the only grass I have," says Suzanne. "All the rest is either gravel or planted in a salute to Piet Oudolf."

OPPOSITE: The rustic sink is tumbled petite granite, and the fixtures are made in Belgium in the classic manner.

ABOVE: Locally grown orchids in a brambled shape are lightly arranged in one of Frances Palmer's elegant vessels.

PREVIOUS SPREAD: "My intent was to have something really comfortable and calm with enough interesting art and objects to keep me captivated," says Suzanne. "I could get happily lost in the Sarah Graham drawing or the lines of the petrified sponge any day."

OPPOSITE: "I love the mixture of the light designed by Giancarlo Valle hovering over the Gerald Bland table of stainless steel mixed with the Regency painted chairs," says Suzanne. "It is practical: good for games with my granddaughters or a cozy dinner for four."

"I love the textural quality of the painting by Kinuko Imai Hoffman as I am drawn to collages of all kinds," says Suzanne. "The Moroccan inlaid table is great for drinks and dinner while watching TV from the banquette."

OPPOSITE: "I chose to have contemporary bath fittings with an eighteenth-century painted Swedish cabinet for towels and bath salts," says Suzanne. "I love the contrast of modern and contemporary throughout the house."

ABOVE: The eighteenth-century Italian bench and continental tapestry, along with the wonderfully wacky chinoiserie nightstands, bring interest to this simple, relaxing guest room.

The Reading Room, with its wonderfully comfortable stacked mattresses for sprawling out with a favorite book while taking peeks at the Santa Ynez Mountains right outside. "I love to see that my granddaughters enjoy reading here as much as I do," says Suzanne.

At Home with

• • • ● • • •

Michael Trapp

• • • ● • • •

The directions from my house are deliciously simple: It's only about thirty minutes from my home in northwest Connecticut and I'm at Michael Trapp's eponymous design store. An interior designer, landscape architect, and antiques dealer, Michael purchased the grand building on April 2, 1990 ("I had a fear of buying on April first," he says).

The shop's simple 1830s Greek Revival facade belies its exotic interior: to enter is to be transported to a place containing the aristocratic grace of southern Italy, along with dashes of faded southern charm. No matter that I'm still in the same state; I suddenly feel very far away.

One enters through the store's first-floor rooms, a labyrinth filled with treasures Michael has brought back from his far-flung adventures over the years: shell necklaces from Papua, French butterfly collection boxes, a seventeenth-century China trade shipwreck jar. Just beyond, I get a glimpse of the villa-style garden that blooms from spring to fall, and into the lower garden where I see a lap pool framed in heavy French limestone with an Italian fountain at one end.

"I want to go to there," I think, but am unsure how, until Michael nods his head toward a secret door that disappears into the frayed patina of a wall he painted to look like old plaster. Necessity was the mother of invention: "I had to disguise the door from the store to the residential part because too many customers were literally walking into my house and exploring," he says, in a way you know it wouldn't bother him if they still did. And who could blame them? The arched windows, designed by the renowned turn-of-the-twentieth-century architectural firm of McKim, Mead & White, cast soft light onto the wall of antique Portuguese tiles by the stove depicting *The Last Supper*.

Upstairs, which Michael uses for guest quarters, he has created decor he describes as being part Medici, part Beauport, Henry Davis Sleeper's fancifully mischievous home perched on the harbor in Gloucester, Massachusetts. Michael has tented the ceiling and covered the walls with golden eighteenth-century Imperial Chinese fabric, bordering it all with seventeenth-century red Italian fringe. The bathroom boasts a nineteenth-century zinc Napoleonic campaign tub. I am tempted to use it, until Michael beckons me to follow him to his actual home, a fifteen-minute drive away.

Before we enter his late-eighteenth-century eyebrow colonial, which sits along a quiet country road, we tour the two dairy barns on the property he's converted to an Aladdin's cave of storage: instead of cows, now rows and rows of stacked crates contain everything from first-century Roman cornerstones to seventeenth-century tapestries, all found "anywhere my whim and the wind will take me."

We enter the house's enormous living and entertaining space. Lunch of grilled cheese is served, and Michael's partner, Michael Meller (a stellar equestrian who has just arrived from a riding competition), joins us under the soaring twenty-foot ceiling. All this mental wanderlusting has made me ravenous, but my appetite is temporarily usurped by the massive whale skeleton from a defunct natural history museum in Indonesia that is suspended above our heads, as if stolen from a Salvador Dalí dream. "I built the room to accommodate it," Michael explains proudly, while handing me a glass of rosé.

Just beneath it hangs a midcentury Hispano-Moresque candelabra. As the afternoon sun pours in through the surrounding long divided windows, we all seem to bask in a glow even without its fourteen lit candles.

Along the exposed back wall hang two still-lifes by a Flemish painter who lived in Spain during the seventeenth century. On the other walls, floor to ceiling, hang blue-and-white seventeenth-century Ming Swatow plates rescued from a shipwreck discovered off the coast of Sumatra ("I bought them all!" says Michael). I can only imagine their stories.

"I am attracted to beautiful things," says Michael, pouring me another glass of rosé. "I love them for what they are, not for their value or pedigree." I realize that Michael isn't only a constant and devoted collector, but also an explorer.

··•●•··

PREVIOUS SPREAD: Michael and I sit under a nineteenth-century Spanish chandelier surrounded by walls covered in Ming Swatow (sixteenth-century ceramics produced in China for the export trade) along with eighteenth-century textiles in the great room at "The Barn," his late eighteenth-century roadhouse in northwest Connecticut.

OPPOSITE, TOP LEFT: Hidden treasures are waiting to be discovered behind the library facade. "Originally it was intended to house the pool equipment, but the builders made it bigger and much too nice for the equipment," says Michael. "So I filled it with old egg collections, along with head hunters' spears and plaster cast footprints."

OPPOSITE, TOP RIGHT: In the guest quarter's kitchen behind the shop, a seventeenth-century Portuguese depiction of *The Last Supper* covers the wall above the kitchen sofa.

OPPOSITE, BOTTOM RIGHT: Cabinets filled with textiles from Iran, Turkish tribes, North Africa, and central Asia in the barn next to the main house.

OPPOSITE, BOTTOM LEFT: In the shop's kitchen under a blowfish is a nineteenth-century plaster of the Venus de Milo with the breasts removed to make it more male.

OPPOSITE, MIDDLE LEFT: The lap pool below the shop tricks you into thinking you've stepped into a sleepy villa somewhere in Italy rather than West Cornwall, Connecticut. "I wanted a lap pool for therapy to heal my back, which I broke while building the stone walls in the garden," says Michael.

PREVIOUS SPREAD: In the dining area in Michael's home, a whale skeleton, which was deaccessioned from a natural history museum in Indonesia, seems to still swim above the French dining room table. The Ming blue-and-white plates were found off the coast of Sumatra and cover the walls in this new section of the house. On the left side of the great room, seventeenth-century Dutch still lifes hang on what was the old exterior (of the original 1790 structure).

THIS SPREAD: In the upstairs living room in the guest space above Michael's shop, the walls are covered in eighteenth-century Imperial Chinese saffron silk with seventeenth-century red silk fringe as trim. A pair of nineteenth-century columns found in his hometown of Cincinnati give the illusion that they are supporting the billowing room. The seventeenth-century walnut schrank is from Augsburg. "I was shopping Brimfield years ago and saw the door in the back of a truck. I had an idea of what the rest was like, so I bought it sight unseen," says Michael.

Stacey and I were lucky to be ushered through the secret door in the back of Michael's shop, which is like traveling to a faraway land and time. In the foyer, a gilt bronze chandelier hangs above an eighteenth-century stone table. The nineteenth-century black-and-white Parisian tiled floor was found in a stone yard on the Île-de-France.

ABOVE: At the guest house above the shop, Egyptianesque columns and sixteenth-century lace soften and frame the bed. Eighteenth- and nineteenth-century paintings adorn the walls.

OPPOSITE: An end table serves a cozy corner next to the bed. "I watch eagles fly above the river as I have my coffee in bed in the morning," says Michael.

FOLLOWING SPREAD: In the kitchen at the guest house that's nestled behind his West Cornwall shop, arched windows removed from the state capital of Rhode Island, designed by McKim, Mead & White, let the afternoon light pour in across a seventeenth-century white stone table. The Ming fish bowl is just the thing in which to display little treasures.

Curtains created from the shawls of
Bhutanese monks in Nepal, trimmed
in seventeenth-century Italian silk lace,
frame the French-style zinc tub and
window seat in the apartment above
the shop. "I love their timeless beauty,"
Michael says.

At Home with

•••●•••

David Netto

•••●•••

If I had any apprehensions that David Netto's iconic glass house built by famed architect Richard Neutra would feel more slick movie-set backdrop than cozy home to a family of four, I was immediately disarmed—if not charmed—by the plethora of Halloween decorations cascading down the sloped front lawn that overlooks Silver Lake Reservoir. "I wanted to show Beverly Hills we could go for it on the east side," quips David, walking past a fog machine to greet us as our Uber driver attempts to navigate the tricky turn around Neutra's Place narrow cul de sac.

David went to architecture school and has since become a prolific designer (both of furniture and interiors), as well as writer who can wax poetic about the work of François Catroux as easily as he can jump two times your height (and later does) on his family's outdoor trampoline.

While his house's decor is very much ready for its close-up, with its design-star cast featuring interior icons such as Le Corbusier, Jens Risom, Jean Arp, and Donald Deskey (a stunning Mies van der Rohe daybed outstretched in the main living area is actually an impostor because David couldn't find the real one in white), its pedigree doesn't dictate the day-to-day narrative of its occupants, who crave surfing as much as they do sketching.

The dazzling open house plan allows you to see both outside and inside almost no matter where you turn, so both nature and human-made creations beckon simultaneously in a deliciously overwhelming way. David's office bookshelves tempt immediate inspection, with subjects ranging from Jacques Grange to *Architectural Digest*'s *Celebrity Homes*, but then again so do the sun-drenched courtyards with creeping fig clinging to their chalk-white walls. The Turner Classic Movies channel continually projects black-and-white Hollywood magic from the modest television screen in the glamorously snug primary bedroom (John Ford's *My Darling Clementine* was playing when we were there) and is a fitting visual catalyst to the facing wall, which is painted bright red and hosts a gallery of snazzy artwork, including a framed drawing by then three-year-old daughter, Kate (who is now nineteen), as an anniversary gift from his director-producer wife, Liz.

At just 1,300 square feet spread out on different levels, the floor plan doesn't try to explain itself, but rather reveals its functionality and glamour as you explore it. There's a wonderful insouciance to how David has mined every nook to make it all work, whether for a children's birthday party or a client meeting.

Coming from chilly Connecticut, Stacey and I are immediately envious of the hive of exterior environments that reinforce the California dream of round-the-clock outdoor living. Here's the perfect patio table to sit à deux for breakfast; there's a fire pit for making s'mores at night, and stepping stones to skip over the carp pond at any hour you please. A flight of stairs leads up to the topmost level, where a simple garage houses a Bentley Brooklands and a Ducati Monster with custom racing kit.

One imagines what it must be like to soar through the Los Angeles streets at sunset in either of these vehicles, knowing that this one-of-a-kind place awaits your return.

But David hasn't made anything too precious here. And because of that, your mind skips ahead to imagining the final and most important scene in the home movie: sitting down to a family dinner and good conversation. This is perhaps what Neutra dreamed for in his creation most of all.

··●●··

PREVIOUS SPREAD: "We use the well-known art of deception to trick the mind into thinking the nook is larger than it actually is," says David. "The mirrored wall allows you to feel like you're engaged with the entire space and not just cornered in."

OPPOSITE, TOP LEFT: "I carry a briefcase to work every day," says David, who travels back and forth from New York to his Los Angeles office in Highland Park. "It's one an old lawyer in London would own. I started with just a toothbrush and a Walkman. It's now always loaded with project material, my laptop, and maybe still a toothbrush."

OPPOSITE, TOP RIGHT: Surfboards belonging to David's daughter Madelyn are at the ready in the back courtyard. Madelyn takes these out to the local beaches in Malibu or the South Bay, all accessible by a short drive west.

OPPOSITE, BOTTOM RIGHT: Post-shoot, David and I have some jumps on the trampoline in his backyard. "It helped me raise two daughters in this house," says David. "There's no age requirement for the trampoline. We've had plenty of adults fall into their youth on this thing."

OPPOSITE, BOTTOM LEFT: This is a sculpture by the late artist Jean Arp titled *Torse-profil*. "It's an exquisite piece that moves from room to room when needed," says David. "It just elevates everything when it makes its entrance."

OPPOSITE, MIDDLE LEFT: "We all should know the man behind these great builds," says David, of Richard Neutra, the Southern California–based modernist architect who built his own 1,300-square-foot glass Silverlake home back in 1959. "Neutra's Los Angeles homes really emphasize a multifunctional space, ready and willing for any adaptation life throws at you and yours."

PREVIOUS SPREAD: "With Europe being so prevalent in these furnishings," says David, "we wanted to add an American flair with a pair of Eames chairs, obviously in red, to give some pop of color to our beautiful but neutral tones throughout the living room."

THIS SPREAD: The outdoor terrace is really part of the living room itself. "The glass wall doesn't stop you from feeling like you're connected with the outside," says David. "This is especially true at night, when I need to decompress, read a book, or browse the auctions."

OPPOSITE: "Nothing is more satisfying than a good African stool or sculpture," says David, who along with Liz found some of these pieces while traveling through Africa. "You'll find this ode in many of my projects, like the Park Avenue or Nashville houses."

FOLLOWING SPREAD: "When you think of a Neutra house, you think of an immaculate environment—crisp and precise," says David. "This family home is filled with novelties and memorabilia, and you see it still works."

OPPOSITE: A Nanna Ditzel hanging egg chair with the whole beloved crew and a Cappellini light blue cabinet in the background. "Simplicity ought to play front and center, however, something warm and fuzzy should always be going on in a kid's room," David says.

ABOVE: David and Liz's daughter's tchotchkes and mementos. The yellow giraffe is a crowd favorite. "Madelyn got this when she was three. She's now fourteen years old, just like that," says David.

At Home with

···•◉•···

Martin Cooper
and
Karen Suen-Cooper

···•◉•···

He replies to my inquiry with the text:

"LET'S CONNECT SOON
—ALWAYS WITH JOY, MARTIN"

I had reached out to Martin and his family about Stacey and me coming to film their Hudson Valley home after seeing it practically glow (it is called B'ellow after all, for its "Big Yellow" buttery glow) in the pages of *Elle Decor* magazine a few weeks prior.

His text a few days later caused me to fumble for a moment. Who is this? Then I realized, it's Martin Cooper, of The Punctilious Mr. P Place Card Co., who, along with his wife, Karen, instinctually practice what they preach, whether via their old-fashioned customized place- and notecards in their exclamatory business, or through modern technology, hence his delightful text.

To speak with Martin and Karen even on the phone is to love their lyrical and compassionate way of thinking and living. They make setting up a shoot feel like a special occasion. But to visit them (along with their eleven-year-old son, Pax) at their Federal-style farmhouse in the Hudson Valley, where they've been living full-time since leaving Manhattan, is to really understand the Coopers. The trio's philosophy is as seamlessly intertwined as their house's history, which comprises a 1790s building, a Federalist front section from 1810, an Italianate wing built in 1870, and a 1920s addition. The rooms, which they've filled with sensual colors and finds from their travels, are meant to evoke daily passages of time and light.

While Karen prepares an organic spread of baba ganoush, quinoa tossed with mesclun greens, and roasted fingerling potatoes tossed with arugula, Pax freestyles on the piano, and Martin ushers me on a tour with his characteristic southern hospitality. The Coopers make everything look effortless, although the journey here was anything but. They oversaw much of the major renovation while living in London. The house had to be taken down practically to its bare bones, due to rot and neglect, before it was built back up again. "Our intention," says Martin, "was to renovate, of course, but also bring the house into its own symmetry while fulfilling our own sense of history."

Walking through the rooms, you feel like you could be anywhere at any time, and yet only here. The Coopers are as wonderfully timeless with their style of dress as with their decor. They both did major stints in the fashion industry, he at Burberry and she with her own luxury brand SUENCOOPER; they are the first couple to be inducted into the CFDA. You can never pinpoint anything at B'ellow to a trend or time period. It's just distinctly, uniquely all theirs.

In the salon, the rich terracotta color of its wallpapered walls combined with the black moldings is like being coddled by dusk. "The warmth of this paper evokes the sensual setting of the sun," explains Martin. "The lyrical quality of its flora pattern is classical in that Roman fresco kind of way, and represents time and memories to us."

We walk next into the stunning black-lacquered dining room, which feels worlds away from the salon, although only a stone's throw. With its teal ceiling (taking its cues from Grand Central Station's iconic one) and its hand-painted-by-Martin gilt zodiac symbols above the antiqued-glass mirrors, the intention here is clear: dine with inspiration and decorate with joy.

After lunch, we all settle into the yellow living room, with its almost eleven feet of ceiling rimmed with cast plasters of architectural fragments made by master plasterer Peter Hone. "We bought them during the period we lived in London," says Karen, offering me some mint-lemon-lime-infused ice water and a LeSaint handmade chocolate. "They give a certain gravitas that was important as a counterpoint to the femininity of the yellow walls."

As I reluctantly leave, Pax presses into my hands some of Mr. P's lemon-and-chutney jams, handmade in small batches in the Hudson Valley. "It is I who should have brought them all a gift," I think regretfully. But then again, the Coopers always make you feel that the gift of your company is, by far, enough.

··●··

PREVIOUS SPREAD: Because this room faces east and the light enters the house here in the morning, the Coopers wanted to infuse this feeling all through the day and the year with a nod to Nancy Lancaster's famous yellow. The chandelier, which they acquired at Doyle's Auction House in New York, is about as tall as Karen. "One of my happiest days was when the Boston piano arrived from Steinway," says Karen. "Our son is now learning to play it. The rest of the room grew up around this instrument."

OPPOSITE, TOP: Martin, Pax, Karen, and I pose in the entry hall in front of the staircase. For its design, the Coopers studied period details of hand-turned balusters and chose the silhouette of urns as a nod to their passion for classical elements. The skirting brackets are "arted" in for each step at it ascends and turns.

OPPOSITE, BOTTOM RIGHT: The classic Greek red figure pottery, a beloved element from art school days, was the starting point for the feeling of the salon. "It inspired us in choosing the Brunschwig & Fils wallpaper and selecting the black lacquer mantel that complements the pottery and leads the eye to the black lacquer dining room," says Martin.

OPPOSITE, BOTTOM LEFT: "Our centerpieces celebrate herbal greenery through the seasons; it scents the room and flavors the menu," says Martin. The Coalport Geneva china is the wedding pattern from Martin's mother. "Having it with us is like having her near."

FOLLOWING SPREAD: "We wanted the terracotta-colored walls to echo the Greek vases sitting on the mantel, to almost feel like the room was like a giant Greek vase," says Martin of the salon. The Coopers used the flash of gold trim on the crown moldings downstairs, as well as the sisal carpeting, to bring a sense of cohesion throughout the rooms.

In the dining room, the family synthesized their personal experiences and then expressed them through its details: "This room, for us, is the theater of our impressions," says Karen. "Memories of beloved places, palaces, paintings, and parties." Shiny black-lacquer walls are the perfect foil for dinners by fixtures that emit one single lumen of candlelight. "It gives a pre-Edison mysterious quality to the night," says Karen. Mystic references of zodiac symbols in gold gilt invite all guests to connect to the details, as everyone is born under a star sign.

PREVIOUS SPREAD: "We love displaying a bit of earth inside," says Martin, "whether it be via potted herbs, ivy, or green fruits such as sensual grapes, limes, or gourds. It celebrates the bounty and beauty of nature and creates a very chic moment no matter the surface."

OPPOSITE: The rhythmic structure of the Farrow & Ball Broad Stripe wallpaper in green tones offers a transition from outdoor nature to interior space. "We never reupholster furniture we purchase at auction," says Martin. "The chairs and the settee are as we bought them."

OPPOSITE AND ABOVE: The pantry is their secret weapon. "It's our service station when we're entertaining guests in the living room," says Karen. "Stocked with a wet bar and a second dishwasher that's a lifesaver after our guests leave." The antiqued mirrored panels help to optically extend the space and give the millwork a lighter feeling—a technique used by Sir John Soane. "We fell in love with gray!" says Karen. "This room is an homage to the rainbow of gray one finds in Europe, a nuance that Farrow & Ball captures so well."

OPPOSITE: The Coopers used antique mirrors on the closet doors to evoke a patina of time. Hand-blown glass doorknobs from the 1920s, which were from the Plaza Hotel with P's embedded within the glass, serendipitously foretell the future family business of Mr. P.

At Home with

·····•●•·····

Pieter Estersohn

·····•●•·····

That Pieter is a family man is apparent from the moment you pull into Staats Hall, his 1839 home in the Hudson Valley. First, he is in front of its monumental Doric portico, thoughtfully packing up the car with his son, Elio, before driving him back to boarding school once our shoot wraps. Second, he originally discovered and then (for over two years) passionately restored this Greek Revival treasure to be a worthy weekend retreat from Manhattan for both his son and his now-late father, Carl.

And as soon as you enter, the reverence for all things familial continues to resonate. The abstract paintings of his late mother, Betty (created during Pieter's childhood when they lived in London), hang proudly in the majestic living room (all thirty-four feet long and sixteen feet wide of it), their grace almost upstaging his parents' Gio Ponti chairs and matching 1830s Joseph Barry sofas.

In fact, generations of family talent are as seamlessly woven throughout the house as bloodlines. In the studio and gallery upstairs (formerly a ballroom in the nineteenth century, complete with atypical dentil molding), Pieter has manifested the ultimate tribute to their past and present artistic pursuits and passions by display: a wood table his father (a former WWII pilot) had constructed out of mahogany, with tiles of doves his mother had painted with glaze. Above it, Elio's own painting (he is also a photographer) of a giant gold mountain is set inside one of his grandmother's old 1950s frames and hung next to a wool needlepoint Pieter's grandfather recreated from a Matisse painting in Tangier. Nearby is a cluster of Pieter's own photographs—one of his favorites, he points out to me, is the nineteenth-century studio of painter Arkhip Kuinzhi in St. Petersburg, Russia. "I love historic artists' studios," he adds, and I can't help but think that one hundred years from now, someone will look at this very space and feel the same thing.

We take coffee in the glossy all-white sunroom downstairs, where Pieter loves to have breakfast en famille (sitting on vintage Harry Bertoia for Knoll chairs from his childhood no less) overlooking his extensive agricultural fields, which are still being farmed today. Later, we sit in the library, laden with dozens of books very specific to the history and architecture of the surrounding region (Pieter has become quite the aficionado) along with many of his parents' art books, beneath an 1850s chandelier. Here, he and Elio swap turns on programming choices to watch on the mounted television: "One night it's Bertolucci and another it's Will Ferrell; you have to compromise," says Pieter affably.

Stacey is a bit intimidated shooting interiors in the home of such a renowned interiors photographer, but the magic light ultimately seduces her. "The house faces exactly south, so you can tell the time by looking at the sun coming through the windows; at noon, there are precise geometric squares of sunlight on the floors," Pieter proudly points out. While she proceeds, Pieter and I take a stroll outside as he shows where he likes to entertain when weather permits. Eight is his ideal number with mixed generations, and walks in the newly restored picturesque garden (an English landscape tradition brought to this area by A.J. Downing) before dinner are a must.

For a summer barbecue, meals are taken out on a gigantic nineteenth-century rug. Also noted: the enclosed area where they keep four Cayuga ducks and a chicken. "Products of isolation guilt at the beginning of COVID up in the country," he admits. "I acquiesced when Elio told me they were bred in Dutchess County in the 1800s. The history geek in me made an unfortunate poetic connection."

When we return inside, Elio is showing Stacey how the afternoon light is causing his father's sarcophagus-style marble tub to glow. "We looked at a hundred houses before finding this place," Pieter says. "During its extensive renovation, we slept in sleeping bags in front of the fireplace on weekends. Elio says he likes modern design, but I know that he is retaining an appreciation of architecture and preservation thanks to this process." The next generation is clearly ready to take its place.

··•◉•··

PREVIOUS SPREAD: A view into the dining room from the front hall—the plaster in the house is mostly original, with many areas replaced or repaired using lime plaster, duplicating the original material used in the 1830s. The walls were originally going to be painted, but Pieter liked the chalky, dry feeling of the bare surface, which incorporate all of the movement of the trowels applying the plaster. In the dining room he wanted an Etruscan red, so he mixed masses of raw pigment into the plaster to get the right intensity. The 2009 painting of Pieter and his son, Elio, now eighteen, is by Mark Beard.

OPPOSITE, TOP: Pieter and Elio's home, Staats Hall, was built in 1839 by Henry Staats, who was the chairman of the Dutchess County Agricultural Society. Pieter bought the house after a three-year search of more than one hundred homes in the Hudson Valley area. He brought in the marble steps from an 1820s church in Massachusetts that was being dismantled, and they fit in seamlessly, with the correct number of risers. "Sometimes finding the right salvage leads you where you want to go," says Pieter. The front door is painted in Eau de Nil, a hue popular in the 1830s, from Fine Paints of Europe.

BOTTOM RIGHT: A portrait of Pieter's dad, Carl, Elio, and Pieter, captured in an 1830s French frame. The winged shoes, representing the Roman god Mercury, are from a school project of Elio's, where he was tasked with recycling an item from a secondhand shop when he was eleven.

OPPOSITE, BOTTOM LEFT: Pieter keeps books here in his library that are related to the Hudson Valley region and its period architecture, including his own research for his book *Life Along the Hudson: The Historic Country Estates of the Livingston Family*, published by Rizzoli. The sofa belonged to his beloved late parents, and the rug was found while on vacation in Jerusalem.

In the living room, the plaster walls have six pigments mixed in to get a warmer tone. Two 1820s Russian neoclassical chairs are on top of a threadbare Oushak rug with a bronze Grand Tour nineteenth-century table between them. The plaster moldings were repaired using vestiges found in the attic when Pieter bought the house back in 2010; a metal blade was crafted using the old profiles in each room, and then the sections were pulled in three-foot increments and mounted together.

"Like all of the six fireplaces in the house, this one draws perfectly and burns throughout the winter," says Pieter. On top of the Doric mantel are birthday cards painted by Elio, some shields, and an 1830s clock with a small bust of Socrates mounted on top. Above the American gilt mirror is a 1960s painting by Pieter's mother, who was an abstract expressionist and later a color-field painter.

The house's former ballroom is now used as Pieter and Elio's studio, a gallery, and an overflow guest room. The bed hangings are French, Turkish, and American. "I'm still waiting for a period pair of lights for the ceiling!" says Pieter.

FOLLOWING SPREAD: A Dunbar dresser, which belonged to Pieter's parents, flanks a comfy sofa.

ABOVE: The upper-floor landing has an 1830s French oak library table with books Pieter has either photographed or written. Paintings by Pieter's mother, Betty Estersohn, from the 1960s, hang nearby. The brass picture rails at the top were installed around the house so as to be able to switch the paintings around and not destroy the plaster. Pieter stripped the floors of decades of stain and sealer using WOCA, a Danish product, and eradicated all of the orange and yellow often found in pine. "I found a final color that approximates what the floors would have looked like after being cleaned several times a year with lye," he explains.

OPPOSITE: The eleven-foot faux-grained mahogany pocket doors were originally in another room, but now they separate Pieter's bedroom and bath. The tub was the only modern concession besides the kitchen storage, although all the plumbing is still nineteenth century. "It is sistered below within an inch of its life; I had nightmares of getting in the tub and ending up in the basement the first time I took a bath," says Pieter. While shooting an early classical home in Italy, Pieter had seen similar matte white marble wainscoting and decided he liked the texture next to the plaster.

FOLLOWING SPREAD: In the kitchen, a chunky Vermont marble counter and backsplash sit on top of Ikea drawers. Hans Wegner chairs are from Pieter's kitchen growing up in New York City. The Italian rosewood table was previously Elio's desk in their Gramercy Park apartment.

At Home with

•••○•••

John and Rachel Robshaw

•••●•••

To get to John and Rachel Robshaw's, you must go through India to arrive in Connecticut. John and I had played tennis nearby just a few weeks earlier, but I'd never been to the weekend retreat he and Rachel share with their young daughter, Regina. It's only fifteen minutes from my house, and yet as soon as I get out of my car, I worry I have forgotten my passport.

129

I walk past a gazebo that mimics an old palace hotel in India with its blinds and cane sofas (all that is missing are the peacocks), and when I enter the Robshaws' storybook 1840s abode, I can already hear exotic squawks coming from Turkey Bird, their Pionus parrot. John, a renowned textile designer, and Rachel, an accomplished interiors photographer, soon greet me, with Regina in tow.

Inside, everything feels spontaneous and effortlessly styled. The living room has the snug proportions of a Colonial house, yet John has visually expanded it by laying down a dhurrie he designed in a multitude of candy-colored stripes, which jibe harmoniously with what must be the only 1800s colonial fireplace in the world painted a creamy lavender. Artwork from friends is joyously hung on almost every available vertical surface.

Rachel is preparing a lunch of red lentil soup with hummus, olives, and sesame crackers in the kitchen, which, of course, is painted a fearless red. On a wall hang large ceramic plates interspersed with turbans wrapped from John's textiles. "They're the perfect replacement whenever a plate falls and breaks," he says, and pulls one off the wall and places it on my head. It feels as light as a parrot feather.

As we all head into the dining room for a bite before the shoot, I remark on the wonderful fabrics on the walls in various patterns. Rachel explains that they are from the Philippines and have been stapled onto the walls of the dining room because they didn't want to commit to wallpaper. "And we'll just take it down if we get tired of it," John says. But how could they: it's like being cradled in jewel-like colors. A twin pair of built-out bookcase hutches (with their own India-inspired arches) painted in a soft coral house dozens of John's thirty-year-old records (leftovers from his days as a DJ at college), which he still plays.

As we sit down, I notice that various textiles—from vintage Indonesian batiks to Indian trade textiles—have been draped on the backs of the rattan chairs. "It's so much nicer to enjoy them rather than them being in a pile," Rachel says, as John kindly pulls a chair out for me.

We later tour the attached annex downstairs, a former tobacco barn transformed into John's print studio (where he experiments with block printing as easily as he swings a tennis racket). The space has since morphed into a stunning lavender-hued lounge that is part library (complete with mosque-inspired bookcases) and part guest room, thanks to a sleeper sofa and outdoor shower. The upstairs guest room makes Stacey and me wish we didn't live so close by. Swathed (including the ceiling) in John's own parrot wallpaper, it's clearly an homage to their beloved Turkey Bird. The other guest room—painted an intense Caribbean palm green—has been converted into Regina's bedroom, complete with kits on the wall and artwork any adult would crave.

When Stacey is done shooting, we tour the lower gardens, where Rachel has created flowerbeds with irises, peonies, and daylilies, and walkways that ramble down to a stream. The doting parents pose for a portrait with Regina. "I have loved blending so many cultures here," says John. "And we love that our daughter is going to grow up learning from them all."

··•●•··

PREVIOUS SPREAD: Coming into the library, John wanted a cozy spot to have small dinners that felt tucked inside. The shaggy Tulu rugs give an exotic warmth, and the Richard Wrightman campaign chairs are casual but elegant. The Indian tiffin trays in a warm copper fit right in like the perfect guest.

OPPOSITE, TOP LEFT: When John bought the house in 2009, there was a series of pavilions around the lawn that ended up being the perfect spots to hide from the sun, relax, and read, not to mention to set up a little bar.

OPPOSITE, TOP RIGHT: John and Rachel pose with their daughter, Regina, under the blossoms of an apple tree in their backyard.

OPPOSITE, BOTTOM RIGHT: The small half-bath John and Rachel added barely fit, so it was fun to wallpaper it with one of John's cheerful Diba Sapphire patterns. The stone sink is from Michael Trapp. "The mask on the wall Rachel calls 'the Poop God,'" says John. "It is said it's good to have some demons around the house to ward off other demons."

OPPOSITE, BOTTOM LEFT: The studio was an old tobacco barn John used to block print samples before turning it into the library. It also became the home of maharaja portraits that he found in Jaipur, which kept him company as he printed and now do the same when he reads.

PREVIOUS SPREAD: In the library John had the perfect place to hang all of his South Indian and Nepalese masks like they were joining the party. The Aleppo Azure fabric makes the vintage pillows pop in front of a Naga table, which has holes in it for grinding grains. A custom chair John and Rachel made is covered in John's Marmar Kashmir textile.

OPPOSITE: The small entryway into the library covered in straw and leather mats from Morocco can take a beating and still look good. A stout chair from Syria is the perfect place to sit down and take off your shoes. "One of the maharaj paintings greets you as you enter, and I pretend it is a distant relative," says John. "And the copper oil pot is full of upside-down brooms, which don't need watering!"

ABOVE: The Syrian inlay chair has an old fabric John used to make: "While I loved [it], it did not sell, at least only to me! I love deep reds and blues together. The benches I had made for my showroom in New York were perfect as banquettes for more places to perch and combined to create storage, which as we all know old houses don't have enough of. I made a massive striped-wool dhurrie for this room, which is perfect for a country house as it's forgiving and lasts, and lots of colors hide the errant wine spill."

OPPOSITE: The other side of the room has another old Naga table and a chair John made with his vintage striped indigo fabric.

"We call this the Hitchcock Room and hope our guest is not afraid of birds," says John. "I covered this oddly shaped room with our Suka Moss wallpaper, and one of our leftover duvet fabrics was made into curtains." The Bihar headboard is covered in his Aleppo light indigo fabric with a woven rug from the Philippines.

ABOVE: A small guest bath becomes a jungle with John's Kulina Moss wallpaper and a Syrian inlaid sink.

OPPOSITE: "A side guest room was the place to test out this lime green I always wanted to use," says John. "I made a custom dhurrie for this room to pick up on the greens."

The entryway is full of light and fun. John made a block-printed rug for it and then paired it with a fish sign from Japan, one of his favorite places, and a Moroccan chandelier he found on the Lower East Side of Manhattan.

At Home with

...●●●...

Susan and Will Brinson

...●●●...

"Ulysses S. Grant smoked his last cigar when he was once a guest here," Susan Brinson proudly tells me as I step into Stony Ford, the nineteenth-century Greek Revival home she and her husband, Will, have painstakingly renovated and revived, from being their own painters, plasterers, plumbers, wallpaper peelers, garden fence constructors, and even bat relocators. "It's been a hotel, horse track, prestigious horse breeding farm," says Susan. "And now it is our obsession."

In addition to being successful commercial photographers and now gatekeepers of their own online shop touting their favorite things to their fan base, Susan and Will are self-proclaimed avant revivalists, which means, as Susan explains, "we revive the past but in a modern, creative way." We walk over to the dining room table, where a massive camera-ready cheese board has been assembled for our enjoyment. That's how the Brinsons roll: while they love to entertain, they don't wait for special occasions to make every detail special. Nina Simone is playing on their (yes) record player (connected to a vintage Marantz receiver and wireless speakers), and Will is concocting the perfect martini. "I care very much about the mood of the glassware," says Susan. "Will is all about the brand of spirits and how to combine them. His craftsmanship is next level." We allow ourselves a few sips before we begin the tour across the home's more than five thousand square feet and three stories.

While they admit to not being interior designers by profession, the Brinsons haven't let that stop them from bringing Stony Ford's intimidating scale and reputation into the accessibly elegant present day, by mixing vintage finds that pay homage to its past with modern-day pieces that will usher it into the future. Susan is clearly drawn to various hues of strong blues in many rooms and has left the hallways in neutral tones. "This way they can lead to the dramatic spaces," she says. And while they proudly show off all the work they have done—from installing a giant ceiling medallion in the living room to wood paneling, flooring, and wallpaper in the triumphant (and much photographed) downstairs guest bathroom—they are equally excited to take me to rooms that still await to test their patience and skill, empty spaces filled with dust, detritus, and demolition dreams. "We love the transformation of renovation," says Will. "It definitely gets worse before it gets better. And we get dirty to shower only to get dirty again."

We sit down for lunch, and Susan passes their signature ham salad as their dogs, Sugar and Nero, look up hopefully from beneath the table. She adds, "But we wouldn't have it any other way."

··●●··

PREVIOUS SPREAD: "We love cocktail hour in the house, it's become a serious hobby for Will," says Susan. "We use this cabinet as our bar. I love collecting small objects and have little antiques interspersed with bar items. Elements from nature and found branches give it that extra height on top."

OPPOSITE, TOP LEFT: "Bringing this American house back to its former glory is our lifelong goal," says Susan. She and her husband, Will, have patiently and lovingly been restoring Stony Ford, their 1850 Greek Revival home in the Hudson Valley, since they purchased it in 2013.

OPPOSITE, TOP RIGHT: "Since college I've loved the decorative arts and pattern," says Susan. "Using Gracie wallpaper in our home combines that love of history and the decorative arts. This design was a re-creation of a vintage Gracie wallpaper, now aptly named after our house, Stony Ford. The vignettes we've created in the house are a combination of the photographer and stylist in us, and a love for telling a story with objects we've collected."

OPPOSITE, MIDDLE RIGHT: A small corner shelf in the guest bathroom is a place for curious objects. Some of Susan and Will's favorite finds in their home now inspire their website, House of Brinson, where they sell similar vintage pieces and collectibles sourced from all over the world.

OPPOSITE, BOTTOM: The Brinsons painted the original fireplace and its surroundings in a light blue-gray, which sometimes leans greenish depending on the time of day. "I always like to break the structure of the fireplace molding with organic arrangements that contrast," says Will.

FOLLOWING SPREAD: The living room is where Susan and Will gather and entertain the most. "The living room was also the biggest challenge for us to figure out the furniture arrangement," says Will. "We're constantly learning and rearranging this space. At first I was unsure about the fluid nature of it, but now I quite enjoy reinventing the space and how we use it."

ABOVE: Rather than let the massive radiators take up space, the Brinsons simply added marble to the top, which now acts as a shelf for curiosities.

OPPOSITE: "Our house is a combination of furniture we've collected as well as inherited from our parents, grandparents, and friends," says Susan. "My mom bought this settee at a yard sale. It's beautifully carved and fits in this nook perfectly."

FOLLOWING SPREAD: "Our main goal when moving into the house was making it livable," says Will. "This room is a great example of a space that will change as we refine the design." The rustic table and Thonet chairs are from the couple's NYC loft and will eventually be replaced with something more suitable for the house. "We like to live in the house, so we understand what the house needs," says Will. Susan made the double-lined drapes that help with the draft from the original windows.

"I wanted the bedrooms to be dramatic jewel boxes," says Susan. "You walk in the room from the hallway, which is a neutral color, and the bedroom wraps itself around you. Bedrooms should be quiet and relaxing spaces, and I think a dark color adds that sense of comfort and warmth." Susan and Will painted the ceiling a slightly different color to lift the room. Susan's mother, Brenda, helped sew all the drapery in the room.

"We renovated this bathroom in six short weeks and did all the installations ourselves, mainly to save money," says Will. The duo chose unlacquered brass for all their finishes to match the antique music note P trap and brass legs that were part of the sink that came with the house. The show-stopping floor is from New Ravenna in their Euclid stone mosaic pattern. It goes back to ancient Greece and was also the most popular quilt pattern in 1850.

At Home with

•••●•••

Alexandra Champalimaud

•••●•••

Even though it is late in the New England fall and her lakeside family compound is void of the usual throng of multiple generations of family and dogs skirting between its buildings overlooking a pristine, private lake, Alexandra Champalimaud's retreat still resonates with the glorious ghosts of past gatherings. Originally, it was a 1920s summer getaway for adults and then a children's camp, until the 1980s, when Alexandra and her husband, Bruce Schnitzer, rescued it. They began to rehabilitate it in the early 1990s, making it the gathering place for their own family milestones. "We've had four weddings here, plays, local rock band concerts, and a lot of skinny dipping," says the Portuguese-born designer, whose Anglo-Portuguese accent has a way of making every word sound delicious and meaningful.

"We've had as many as fifty people sleeping here," Bruce chimes in proudly, as their three black English cocker spaniels follow us through the house's bright bottle-green doors. In the entry, a simple wood wall painted burgundy is the backdrop for mounted fallen antlers, wooden cutouts in tribute to large catch-and-release salmon and one papier-mâché giraffe head. A cigar store Native American figure in one corner surveys the expected assortment of simple birch furniture, fishing rods, a couple of canoe paddles, all-weather boots, and jackets. This family is ready to seize the day no matter the weather.

The interior's decidedly functional yet cheeky decor is both streamlined and cheerful: it nods to the past and winks toward the future. "It's an effort to give the appearance of having done nothing, but with moments of chic, but natural, decorations," explains Alexandra, as we walk through the cavernous former children's theater, which is now a living area used for large events when needed, but usually might more aptly be called a family playspace.

On one side is a small Shakespearean stage, painted to resemble the Globe Theatre, with a portrait of the Bard, all created by campers of yesteryear. The spirit of performance is still going strong, with evidence of a drum set, a piano, a life-size papier-mâché cow that was a prop for a family wedding, and a colorful Welcome to Camp Kent paper banner created by the current generation of grandchildren. Facing the stage is a giant stone fireplace and minimal furniture (unless a foosball and a Ping-Pong table count): a fancifully curved white sofa (left over from a movie shoot), an indestructible coffee table, and a chrome and cowhide sling-back chair from Bruce's 1970 bachelor's apartment. Overhead, draped flags represent the range of family members' origins, hailing from Canada, Portugal, Belgium, France, England, Switzerland, Norway, and Texas. It reinforces the collective spirit of how anywhere in the world can feel like home, as long as it is shared with those we make room for at our table.

At the far end is the giant stage, beneath which are suspended giant red candleholders that were made by Robert Isabell, the late party planner extraordinaire, for Alexandra and Bruce's wedding in 1995 that took place in their main residence, a historic eighteenth-century home (built by one of the signers of the Declaration of Independence) in nearby Litchfield. These lanterns were moved to the theater for Alexandra's eldest son's wedding and have found a permanent home.

Alexandra ushers us into the kitchen (originally the backstage area for theater performances) for a lunch of homemade tomato soup, roast chicken, and local white corn on the cob. Gracing the walls in bold bright colors is a graffiti-like mish-mosh of former campers' names now supplemented by entries of the couple's friends and family. Over the years, guests found worthy of having made some useful contribution to the camp life are encouraged to add their names to the kitchen decor. It's so much more inviting that any paint color could ever be.

While Alexandra is known for renovating luxurious hotels around the world, this place clearly embraces her true self. As we have dessert of poached pears and ice cream out in the gazebo with its views of the lake (where she swims every summer morning), Bruce links his arm around Alexandra's shoulder to say goodbye; she whispers something in his ear, and he smiles. Then he and the dogs take their leave to allow us to begin the business of our shoot. But my head is elsewhere. It longs to be with this family, to see them gather for life's big and small moments and pleasures. This is an ideal life, I think. Not because it's perfect, but because it is so personally celebrated.

··●●··

PREVIOUS SPREAD: The kitchen, which was the backstage area of the former 1920s summer camp, still sports the names of former campers as they awaited their turn in the spotlight. Now it is a backdrop for generations of family gatherings. "Pellegrino and red wine are always a staple here," says Alexandra.

OPPOSITE, TOP: "We have retained the original bones and have barely touched the interiors," says Alexandra of her design philosophy. "Ugly is perfect here and beautiful to us."

OPPOSITE, MIDDLE, RIGHT: The Shakespearean stage is original to the former summer camp.

OPPOSITE, BOTTOM RIGHT: Over the years, Alexandra and Bruce have encouraged their friends and families to add their names to the wall as well. "It's a visual representation of Camp Kent's history and journey to becoming our family home," says Alexandra. "You can only add your name if you have contributed substantially to the basic restoration of the theater."

OPPOSITE, BOTTOM LEFT: Susanna and Alexandra pose in the entry under "The Wall of Warring Salmons." The back wall shows the collection of trophies, which have been the fruit of family adventures. The two most important ones are partially covered—two Atlantic salmon that were caught and released. "Happily, I won this competition," says Alexandra. "Mine was a thirty-six-pound female, Bruce's a thirty-three-pound male."

OPPOSITE, MIDDLE, LEFT: "Foosball is a contested activity in our family," says Alexandra. "It's a part of the Camp Kent indoor decathlon!"

PREVIOUS SPREAD: "This magnificent room fits hundreds of people and is really an homage to our family represented by their individual nations and flags," says Alexandra.

ABOVE: "Through this window you will see that our house looks over one of Connecticut's lovely small lakes," says Alexandra. "I often swim what is half a mile each way. This room in particular often serves as a bar when we're entertaining."

OPPOSITE: "The tap room is the best place to be in the autumn as we are not insulated," says Alexandra. "Some years ago, we allowed friends to use the theater as a stage set for a small movie. As a thank-you they left behind this rather charming '60s sofa that was part of the set."

"All found pieces, including some from my own collection, make it very much our own space," says Alexandra. "The green table came from the old camp, which we salvaged and painted bright green. The floor lamp has been, and forever will be, crooked."

OPPOSITE: The poster comes from the college collections of Alexandra's son. The branches are native to the property and are artistically tied to frame the space."

ABOVE: "The Georgian sideboard and ice-fishing chairs are pieces we love and have nowhere else to place; they get distributed throughout the house," says Alexandra. The sailboat was a gift to Alexandra's son from the father of one of his early girlfriends.

At Home with

•••●•••

Alex Papachristidis

•••●•••

It's not every day you pull into a sweeping driveway—even in the Hamptons—and are greeted by a monolithic über white sculpture of a tree. Fashioned by the famed Ugo Rondinone out of cast aluminum, with its base framed by an immaculately clipped real-life boxwood hedge, the tree's branches curl against the tidy backdrop of the cedar-shingle Georgian-style weekend home of designer Alex Papachristidis, precisely projecting what its gracious host intends: welcome home and expect fantasy.

By fantasy I don't mean anticipating the unreal. I mean fantastically receiving what we all secretly dream of as weekend guests: to be pampered, dazzled, embraced, and loved by someone who believes as much in dressing for family dinners as he does in wearing pajamas at breakfast. By someone who chooses the most luxurious of Fortuny fabrics in which to upholster the enormous sectional sofa in their media room, while insisting that young children and dogs are as welcome on it as much as napping adults.

The first thing I notice as I cross the stenciled threshold is the skirted octagonal table outfitted with stacks of design books and Chinese lotus bowls filled with nuts and barbecue potato chips. Clearly, Alex and his longtime partner, Scott Nelson, don't want guests to pass through the front door and go more than two feet without being offered something delicious.

"Hi, baby doll!" Alex's customary greeting always makes me melt under the light of his cheerful optimism. He sees me eyeing the chips and immediately hands me the bowl, hugging me with his free arm. He is ready to feed, educate, or gossip, and often all three things happen at once. "The table is custom," he answers in rapid fire when I ask about its provenance, while steering me toward the living room. "Inspired by the Villa Malcontenta outside of Venice. Tell me everything, and do you eat lobster?"

There are things to visually taste as well—sumptuous offerings of leopard-print silk velvets, rich browns, bronzes, and faux bois paper at first glance. "We're the fanciest, most informal people you'll ever meet," he admits, after I tell him how his style leaves me a little breathless.

Staff are efficiently putting the finishing touches on an expansive summer buffet lunch Alex refers to as "salad and fixings," with dozens of filled bowls intended to tempt even the choosiest. Before we sit (with Alex's niece Samantha, her husband, David, and their darling eight-year-old daughter, Elle, who are all housemates), Alex is excited to show me a lacquer box he has just won at auction: he is an insatiable collector, and to prove his point, he opens a former downstairs coat closet he's converted to contain his growing china collection: "I'm eternally shopping," he says. "And I use everything. There's nothing more important to us than gathering friends and family around a beautifully set table. We don't need a special holiday for that. And Elle is always the first one to admire anything new!"

After lunch, when I ask to go for a walk on the beach only moments away, Alex complies with his customary cheer, but we don't get too far. I could walk for miles oceanside, but after a few minutes I can sense Alex longing to turn home. For him, rare relaxation is best spent playing Biriba, a Greek card game, with his beloved sister Ophelia (who lives close by on the beach with her husband, Bill, in a house Alex designed for them) against Scott and Samantha.

I am happy that I don't play cards, if only to give me private time to luxuriate in my guest room, which is outfitted like a five-star hotel, if that hotel was run by the best friend you never get to spend enough time with. A giant clutch of roses ("Always fresh flowers everywhere, whether we have guests or not!" confirms Alex) has been placed by my bedside, along with a pad and pen to jot down dreams or errands, a box of "tissue necessaire" (invented by Alex's best friend, Harry Slatkin's brother, Howard), and a glass of bottled water. Even though it's only two o'clock, I climb in between the Porthault sheets and pull the delicious custom Clarence House paisley bedspread up to my chin.

Then I hear, "Suz?" It's Alex calling me to a game of tennis on their court, and afterward we sip iced tea in the pool house, brackets holding a collection of blue-and-white porcelain vases spread out on the wall behind us and flanked by two nineteenth-century Italian stone statues Alex found at the New York Botanical Gardens benefit.

Just before dinner, we stroll (always with Alex's Yorkshire terrier, Teddy, trotting by his side or in the crook of his arm) across the lush lawn and pause to chat by the outdoor spaces he's created with oversize sculpture: Claude Lalanne's bronze apple and a serene face by Igor Mitoraj.

A wind picks up, and a row of white hydrangeas bend their swollen heads in the gentle evening breeze. Candles are being lit inside the dining room as we turn toward home. "You know the most important thing about living here," Alex tells me, "is that I know Elle will carry our collected love for this house into the next generation."

··●··

PREVIOUS SPREAD: Alex and I take a stroll through his family's garden of delights, complete with its own Claude Lalanne apple from Paul Kasmin.

OPPOSITE, TOP LEFT: "We keep the garden parklike," says Alex. "The only flowers are the white hydrangea planted in the back of the house, and from here we can admire them whenever we have lunches and dinner outside."

OPPOSITE, TOP RIGHT: Alex and I posing in his living room during teatime among the multigenerational collections of objects and furniture.

OPPOSITE, MIDDLE, RIGHT: "I always love to have a buffet of salads so everyone gets what they want," says Alex. "We love to offer fixings full of choices for all the different generations of family tastes. And everything looks better when served in blue-and-white bowls from Mottahedeh."

OPPOSITE, BOTTOM: The Igor Mitoraj sculpture makes for wonderful punctuation among the fourteen-foot-tall sculpted hedges surrounding the family's garden.

A stylish signature of Alex's decorating is stenciled floors, and the entry to his own house is no exception. "We love it because it is so simple to maintain with pets and guests," he says.

OPPOSITE: Because of his passion for blue-and-white dishes around the house, Alex used delft tiles in the fireplace surround in the dining room.

ABOVE: "There's nothing I love more than entertaining at home," says Alex. "Collected and layered table settings are my greatest joy. And I always use local vendors to do my flowers and plants."

In the dining room, a bookcase styled like a cabinet of curiosities showcases gilded lions, shells, gilt bronze ormolu, coral, and eighteenth-century porcelain.

ABOVE: When I spent the night in the downstairs family guest bedroom, Alex had ensured that no detail was forgotten: "We believe that a guest should be surrounded by beauty, luxury, and comfort."

OPPOSITE: The sunroom facing the swimming pool offers an ideal place for an afternoon nap or reading. Alex found the snail in an antique show in the Hamptons. The floral wallpaper is from Cowtan & Tout, and the daybed is covered in a tobacco textile from Clarence House. "I love mixing patterns and prints throughout my house," says Alex.

At Home with

·••●••·

Darren Henault

·••●••·

How fun to fall down the rabbit hole of Darren Henault's Hudson Valley retreat! This former Christmas tree farm with an 1800s house is now delightfully populated by thirteen-year-old twin girls named Bunny and Lulu and a French Bulldog named Tuck, and has a storybook effervescence from the get-go. Orchestrating all of it with a kind of Willy Wonka delight is their parent and our host, designer Darren Henault, who has revamped every inch with nods to the past that are equal parts cheeky and reverential.

As soon as we arrive, we are offered coffee on the Greek Revival porch and bask in Darren's ability to create outdoor rooms as sumptuous as indoor ones. The twins flutter by in crisp tennis whites, having just come back from a lesson at the nearby Millbrook Golf and Tennis Club, and invite us to follow them as they make grilled cheese sandwiches along with "Big Daddy," Darren's partner, lawyer Michael Bassett. (Darren is known as "Little Daddy.")

As we watch the girls press melted gruyère onto home-made sourdough bread, I realize that their kitchen embodies the unique spirit, not just of the house, but of the whole property: its beautifully detailed traditional cabinetry in cream is solidly rooted in design history, but its pine floor painted with large blue waves makes sure to tell you that unexpected surprises are also in store. "I've always loved a Bunny Mellon painted-floor moment," says Darren, handing me half of a warm sandwich, "but I certainly didn't want perfection or anything to look too new."

To his point: in the bathrooms he's used footed tubs rather than installing big built-in bathtubs and unlacquered brass fixtures throughout ("as I knew they would tarnish within weeks and look old"). The oak used in the garden room (with its heated floors and plump eighteenth-century chaise longue I instantly covet for a nap) is reclaimed. The sofa cushions are all feather and down, so they look rumpled after someone's been sitting in them. "That's appealing to me," Darren says.

Nor does he want to live in a museum: all of the art in the house is contemporary, culled from various artists Darren and Michael have met over the years. "And we've got instant hot water and lots and lots of it," he says after showing us one of the splendid guest bathrooms, complete with couture linen covering its walls. "All of the house's systems have been brought up to modern technology. It looks old, but it works like new!"

The house's layout is charmingly deceptive, as Darren and Michael have added onto its back and far side, so when you approach, it first appears as a modest farmhouse. It's only when you start walking through it that you realize how many rooms there are to explore. "It isn't big," says Darren. "But it evolves."

Later we stroll across the fifty-three-acre grounds to visit the chicken coop, apple orchard, beehives, flower garden (where we clip dozens of dahlias), and the casual pool area, complete with a wood pergola and a massive linden tree that offers the perfect amount of shade. Along the way, we decide to pose for our joint portrait on the round limestone balls that Darren has found at an estate sale and then mounted on stone bases in the grass to complete an allée-like formation. "I get a lot of compliments on my balls," he says with a grin.

After we wrap the shoot, Darren takes us to visit Rizzel, his new horse, newly arrived from Ireland. "He's half Connemara and half thoroughbred. He's spunky and game for anything," says Darren. As Stacey and I leave the stable, I take one last look to watch Darren saddle up. He looks as ready to embrace whatever the adventure may bring as his steed.

··●●●··

PREVIOUS SPREAD: "My friend Willa Shalit made the life cast of me when my jaw was still sharp," says Darren. Family photographs layered over the books in the library add depth and texture. "This space is mostly our little snug in the winter."

OPPOSITE, TOP LEFT: Perfect spot for our joint portrait was on the set of limestone balls Darren salvaged from an estate in New Jersey and then mounted on bases. "I like how they draw your eye toward the specimen trees," says Darren.

OPPOSITE, TOP RIGHT: Lulu and Bunny's wagon ready for duty outside the terrace of the former Christmas tree farm.

OPPOSITE, RIGHT, MIDDLE: In the garden room, a bronze sculpture purchased in Florence at the Galleria Pietro Bazzanti & Figlio layers beautifully over the custom iron birdcage that houses zebra finches. "I love how their chatter brings life to the room," says Darren.

OPPOSITE, BOTTOM RIGHT: The carved eagle console with a faux marble top was purchased at John Norwood Antiques. "I rather irreverently cut it down to make it shallower," says Darren. The mirror was found at a flea market in the south of France.

OPPOSITE, BOTTOM LEFT: On the kitchen floor, artist Matt Austin re-created the pattern from a piazza in Lisbon Darren had been obsessed with for years: "I love how it instantly created a whimsical mood."

FOLLOWING SPREAD: Fresh herbs in terracotta pots line the walkway to the mudroom and kitchen.

ABOVE: In the old living room, the black marble fireplace from Chesneys was installed to replace a bad wooden mantel. Its lines are elegantly set off by a pair of Ming dynasty vases and contemporary photography from the Yancey Richardson Gallery. "I like the tension between a softly styled room with the graphic photography," says Darren.

OPPOSITE: "The blue guest room was a study in restraint for me," says Darren. Yards of printed fabric from Les Indiennes is used on the windows, upholstery, and bed drape. The large braided rug was custom-made in Pennsylvania.

In the dining room, the walls were hand-stenciled with a slight sheen but no color, creating a luminescent effect. "I wanted the pattern to be almost invisible," says Darren, "to come and go in the changing light." The solid mahogany dining chairs were painted in Swedish milk paint to keep the room light.

OPPOSITE: An antique wooden valance was shortened to cap the window at the top of the stair landing. The Biedermeier settee was purchased at auction in New York from Doyle.

FOLLOWING SPREAD: The twins' bedroom windows are capped with Orientalist valances that were inspired by the pair of lanterns purchased in Belgium. "I had seen them online and knew immediately they were a perfect jumping-off point," says Darren.

ABOVE, LEFT: Carved balsa wood animal heads from India and a Lee Jofa wallpaper create an outdoorsy mood in the library bath. "I like designing bathrooms," says Darren. "It's a place to combine function with whimsy."

ABOVE, RIGHT: A handmade brass tub imported from Normandy is the centerpiece of the primary bathroom. The marble topped gueridon is a useful table that also "furnishes" the space more like a room.

OPPOSITE: Darren placed the tub in the middle of the girls' nursery for ease at bath time. Then he covered the walls in a Kravet fabric for sound quality.

FOLLOWING SPREAD: A check fabric from Chelsea Editions, rather than wallpaper, was applied to the walls of the main bedroom, specifically to give the room a handcrafted feel. The checks aren't painfully straight. The bedding is from Matouk. The photo of the girls expresses personality rather than beauty. "It makes me laugh every time I look at it," says Darren.

At Home with

Kate Brodsky

We are always cranky about driving from Connecticut to the Hamptons to shoot a house, as there's no easy way to get there, no matter what time you leave and what path you take. But it's impossible not to feel immediately happy when you pull up to Kate Brodsky's historic 1901 getaway in East Hampton.

Perhaps it is the profusion of flowers as soon as you walk in the door: whether via the chic chintz patterns cascading across furniture in the expansive living room, or the painted blossoms and greens growing across the dining room's customized mural wall, or, by way of the real kind—of Queen Anne's lace, asters, and Japanese anemones plucked from Kate's own garden and casually clutched into bouquets everywhere.

Or . . . it's all that delicious color that elevates one's mood if not pulse: a raspberry pink-and-white checkerboard floor in the sunroom, juicy lime green on the brazenly bare floors, and the explosion of cherry reds in the kitchen.

But it's our host who is really setting the ebullient tone. She has, after all, masterminded every inch of the place and runs it with the charismatic ease of a professional who owns KRB, one of Manhattan's most sought after design emporiums, and she's also mother to three charming girls under the age of thirteen.

It's in her DNA, of course. We had already filmed her mother, design doyenne Suzanne Rheinstein, at her stately Hancock Park home in Los Angeles a few years earlier, and just crossing her daughter's threshold, we can see how Kate has inherited and reinterpreted Suzanne's gracious and elegant spirit to call her own on the East Coast: the porch ceilings painted in pale pink instead of the expected blue, a traditional rolled-arm sofa extending to an exuberant seventeen feet of length, sleek marbled glaze tiles surrounding a fireplace instead of distinctive delft tiles. And, of course, how Kate uses Suzanne's iconic textile collections throughout the house, patterns Kate grew up with and has now reimagined here.

As her ten-year-old daughter, Freddie, bakes us homemade chocolate chip cookies in between her online math class, Kate takes us through the house's extensive three and a half floors, starting with the lower level's garden room and playroom/TV room for kids. "We love building forts down here!" says Freddie, swooping in to join the tour. The top floor's converted attic has a bunkroom for the girls and their sleepovers. Like the rest of the house, it is bright and cheerful and done all in red, white, and blue, and Kate has glossed the red on the bases of the beds for an extra bit of chic. Along the way is the cozy main bedroom, with its uniquely stenciled floor in gray, buff, and aqua, happily cohabitating with the fireplace mantel in the same aqua, and curtains in spring green. "I really love color and its ability to lift and change your mood as well as soothe your spirit," says Kate.

After lunch on the front porch of salads grabbed from the local go-to Loaves and Fishes, we take coffee on the outdoor porch outfitted in vintage rattan. Perched from here, I can see the pool with its Slim Aarons-worthy custom sludge-green tent with white scallops and a pink ceiling. "We knew we needed a real haven for shade to watch the kids swimming, as they can be here for hours," says Kate. So could I, I think.

Nearby, just off the garden, where the tall dahlias are bending in the soft fall wind, is a stone fireplace where the family loves to make s'mores at night. Stacey and I look at each other after accepting a final cookie. Usually we can't wait to beat the traffic and head back home. However, in this instance, we will make an exception and linger.

··•●•··

PREVIOUS SPREAD: Kate separated the desk she shares with her husband from the rest of the primary bedroom with a pair of vintage rattan etagères.

OPPOSITE, TOP: Kate and Susanna on the front porch with Peaches, a Lagotto Romagnolo. Kate painted the porch floor green as a bridge between the garden and the house.

OPPOSITE, BOTTOM: "Dick Bories and James Shearron were instrumental in helping us turn a wonky 1901 house with no foundation into a lovely, rambling place for a family," says Kate. "I prefer to be in the shade whenever possible— so we had Bories & Shearron design this glam tent for us by the pool. I hide in there and watch the girls swim."

FOLLOWING SPREAD: "This Lee Jofa print on the sofa, Hollyhock, lived in my 'fantasy file' for about a decade," says Kate. "I just love it, especially because flowered chintz is quite forgiving of dirty dogs and children with sandy feet. The Queen Anne chair on the left was in my childhood house, and I really love having the continuity of that in my own house. I painted the floors in the living room and dining room in one of my favorite greens and didn't put down rugs."

The extra-long sofa in the pink sunroom is everyone's favorite. It's great for a nap on a sunny Sunday after lunch or for piling onto while watching a movie on a rainy day.

OPPOSITE: Bob Christian painted the mural in the family dining room. "I told him I wanted it to look like a garden where all the flowers bloomed at once, and that's exactly what he gave me!" says Kate. The marbled glaze tiles on the fireplace surround are new but feel like a fresh take on a delft tile surround. The Regency convex mirror came from Tom Stansbury Antiques.

FOLLOWING SPREAD: In the dining room, an eighteenth-century Dutch black brass chandelier hangs over a vintage Michael Taylor for Baker table. The oversize leaf-green hurricanes are made by Kate's store, KRB, in New York.

Kate wanted the guest room to be pretty enough for when her mother, Suzanne Rheinstein, came to stay. Accordingly, she covered the walls, bed, and windows in Suzanne's Garden Roses fabric for Lee Jofa. Christopher Spitzmiller's Suzanne lamps flank the bed, made with linens from Leontine Linens. A row of Liz Young drawings hangs above the bed.

OPPOSITE: In the downstairs guest bathroom, an initial present of nineteenth-century silhouettes from Kate's mother, Suzanne Rheinstein, started her on the path to a full collection. "I love the way they look hung on this Porter Teleo wallpaper," says Kate. "And I think of my mother every time I see them."

FOLLOWING SPREAD: Lined with beadboard, the third-floor bunk room often hosts sleepovers with friends and cousins. Shades made from Décors Barbares fabric cover the skylights, and Tam Tam lights by Marset are by each bedhead.

At Home with

•••●•••

Charlotte Barnes

•••●•••

Designer Charlotte Barnes is the type of person who, if you are lost, will come out onto the road from her driveway to rescue you. Her warmth and sparkle is visible even from my distant approach. Her home's exterior is equally sparkly—at least metaphorically speaking. The classic American shingle carriage house—complete with turret and horse weathervane—boasts an eight-and-a-half-foot-tall Dutch door painted in Farrow & Ball's iconic Hague Blue. The high-gloss paint finish is topped with a Charles Edwards handmade brass ring knocker.

We follow Hope—her Labradoodle—into one of the most glamorous entries I've ever seen. It's all white, with lacquered walls and ten-foot-high ceilings papered in Venus, a painterly, marbleized-looking, multihued wallpaper. "This room, for me, was a lesson in restraint," says Charlotte. "This house is a downsize from our last, so I wanted to fill each room only with highly edited and beloved pieces that exude a sense of beauty and purpose." Even from the get-go, this space proves her point: a mirrored screen (plucked from Charlotte's own thirty-piece furniture collection), a bronze sculpture (a treasured gift by the artist Sarah Ondaatje), and a painted early-nineteenth-century Swedish table with a marble top, all seem to coexist with the levity of a wonderful dinner party already in progress. "I am a believer in when you buy what you love, you always find a place for it," Charlotte tells me, while ushering me to the nearby bar nook (formerly a closet), which is lacquered in a rich deep navy/black color with brass hands for its door knob. "I've always loved these hands from Charles Edwards," she explains, "and finally I've found the perfect place to put them." She hands me a glass of wine.

The table is set for lunch in the dining area—which has open access to the kitchen and extensive views of the garden of boxwood balls outside—with red wicker mats, white plates, and vintage monogrammed purple napkins. "I started collecting vintage napkins when I lived in London," she tells me. As we enjoy our butternut squash soup and endive salad with fennel and blue cheese, I can't help but be intrigued by a nearby large English secretary. It belonged to Charlotte's late father and is where she loves to write letters on her personalized stationery. "Some people feel that brown furniture is no longer relevant; however, I believe that one should be surrounded by things that they love—period. I don't really care if something is old or new," explains Charlotte. "I like to look at beautiful things, but I also like to use them. It displays pieces I use to decorate my table, and the writing surface doubles as a place to hold things like the wine bucket and water pitcher when entertaining."

We have dessert of lemon bars in the living room and even squeeze in a round of backgammon (on a 1970s chrome-and-glass table, of course), although it's hard to concentrate surrounded by the sumptuous walls covered in a colorfully printed fabric. "It's a true denim blue, which goes with everything," she tells me of the giant paisley design, accented with cream and pops of cranberry. Charlotte has such artful effortlessness in the layering of her rooms: every corner is loved and used and yet remains at its glamorous best. As relaxed as you are here, you want to bring your A-game too, as even the bathrooms feel like

their own mini installations, complete with bold wallpaper and artwork.

Later, we tour the upstairs, and I make a beeline for her dressing room, as I know it will reveal her penchant for fashion (she worked for Ralph Lauren and Pomellato) as well as for jewelry. Indeed, clothes are hanging behind closet doors papered in grass cloth and littered with beloved family photos and paintings. Jewelry from far-flung places (as well as several pairs of Les Bonbons, earrings from her daughter's buzzy jewelry line, Rebecca de Ravenel) is displayed hanging on lampshades, majolica bowls, and silver trays.

Before I head on the road back from Greenwich to my neck of the Connecticut woods, we have a cappuccino on her trellised porch (also all white), complete with a tented roof of yards and yards of striped fabric. "While I was working on a project in Istanbul, I became inspired by their tented rooms," Charlotte recalls. "I wanted a sexy outdoor space where people would love to congregate, so I brought it home and gave it my own American twist." She pauses for a minute. "I think surprises in a house—whether on a ceiling or behind a closed door—are rather wonderful."

··•●•··

PREVIOUS SPREAD: An English secretary holds collected blue-and-white vases and dinnerware. "Not only are they pretty to look at but I use them here in the dining room," says Charlotte. She also writes letters and works on her laptop at the desk.

OPPOSITE, TOP LEFT: Charlotte's extraordinary use of jewel-like colors and exotic patterns makes the ideal portrait backdrop for us.

OPPOSITE, TOP RIGHT: Charlotte's charming carriage house, built in 1889, is updated with her favorite Hague Blue color on the front door and windows.

OPPOSITE, BOTTOM RIGHT: A favorite painting found years ago began the mood in Charlotte's library, painted in Farrow & Ball's Pelt.

OPPOSITE, BOTTOM MIDDLE: A glimpse of Charlotte's closet reveals a mix of collected caftans, ponchos, and coats. "I decorate like I dress," says Charlotte. "A mix of traditional but not."

OPPOSITE, BOTTOM LEFT: On Charlotte's porch, a vintage set of Salterini, which she purchased in Charleston, is paired with a custom-colored China Seas Les Indiennes fabric.

OPPOSITE, LEFT, MIDDLE: Hope, Charlotte's Labradoodle, sits on a custom-colored Knot & Co. stair runner.

PREVIOUS SPREAD: "This is our everything room," says Charlotte. "My inspiration was the iconic room Mongiardino did for Lee Radziwill in London. It's a place where I can mix lots of patterns and colors, furniture and art. The Christopher Spitzmiller lamps add the 'lipstick.' The paper-backed fabric Jamawar is from Penny Morrison. The embroidered textiles were made into pillows bought in Istanbul."

ABOVE: "Closets are a perfect spot to hide the bar," says Charlotte. "It's such a surprise when we open the doors to reveal a shot of color, pretty glasses, and nearly anything to make a drink."

OPPOSITE: "I have been collecting plates and glasses for as long as I can remember," says Charlotte. "I believe the best tables are a mix of different colors and patterns." Her cabinet holds glasses from her grandmother and mother, both vintage and new, from Baccarat to Tiffany, and even Pier 1 Imports.

FOLLOWING SPREAD: "The entry to our house, I would say, is the party room," says Charlotte. "It's got a little bit of glamour right when you open the front door." The walls are a creamy lacquer, and the Florence screen and Walker sofa are from her eponymous furniture collection. The custom rug is a copy of a 1920s rug Charlotte found many years ago. The hand-carved 1950s chair is from Ethiopia.

PREVIOUS SPREAD: "I love to mix in a little Fortuny in nearly every room I do," says Charlotte, who paired Antoinette Poisson on her Carey dining chairs (named after her mother) and Fortuny on her Barrett Stool. The linen curtains are from Claremont with Houlès trim. The dining table is 1940s French. The blue-and-white antique pot Charlotte bought on a trip to Hong Kong on her twenty-sixth birthday doubles as a place to hold the kitchen Christmas tree.

ABOVE: "I covered everything in my dressing room in a vinyl grass cloth from Cowtan & Tout," says Charlotte. "It's easy on the eyes but also to take care of! I have tons of silver picture frames that I have collected over the years and keep my most favorites in this room."

OPPOSITE: The room began for Charlotte with the Quadrille blue-and-white fabric, embroidered bed linens from Julia B., a faux fur throw from Bunny Williams Home, and handmade lampshades to mirror the circles in the fabric. "I always think it's the little things that become so important," says Charlotte.

FOLLOWING SPREAD: Appliqué monogrammed linens, Lyford Pagoda wallpaper from China Seas, and vintage lamps with Vaughan lampshades, all ensure dreams that are sweet and chic.

ABOVE: A Quadrille custom-colored wallpaper in Charlotte's mudroom is the perfect backdrop for all of her (and her dog, Hope's) totes.

OPPOSITE: From Charlotte's own furniture collection, the Balding desk and Gracie mirror were the first things to find their home in this house. She has re-covered the stool "I don't know how many times," and its latest incarnation is in one of Charlotte's favorite Soane stripes. An antique Buddha wears a turban she got in India, with Carolina Irving lampshades on Christopher Spitzmiller Zig Zag lamps. "When I entertain," says Charlotte, "the greens go away and are replaced with candles."

At Home with

•••●•••

Johnson
Hartig

•••●•••

At first I was devastated to learn that Johnson was selling his spellbinding Citrus House in Hancock Park. Stacey and I had filmed there for the series just a few years earlier, and when we weren't swooning over every one of its inventive DIY details (such as his taping rose catalog pictures around his bed posts and lining glass-fronted cupboards with wrapping paper), we were soaking up Johnson's charismatic company.

Whenever we are in Los Angeles for shoots, we always stay with Johnson's neighbor, our beloved friend Timothy Corrigan—a designer and another video series favorite—so I was delighted at least to learn that Johnson had only moved a few blocks from him.

Knowing he was an extreme early riser (who then tucks into a quick late morning nap before heading back to his Hollywood studio just a few blocks away), I called Johnson just as soon as I woke at six a.m., due to my East Coast jet lag, and practically begged if I could swing by and see the new digs. "I'm still knee-deep in decorating this dump," he texted right back.

"I don't care," I wrote back, and headed right over.

It's a joy to walk to something in L.A., especially a house you're excited to see, but within minutes I'm double-checking the address. On a block filled with exposed-brick Grand English Tudor and Mediterranean homes, Johnson's abode is hidden behind a lush canopy of hedges, olive trees, and dozens of potted boxwood topiaries. In fact, one would walk right past its introverted exterior. But suddenly Johnson is here, standing in front of his pink door, holding Flower, his new rescue rat terrier mix. "Come right in," he says with a kind of Willy Wonka mysterious smile. He's sporting a pair of Libertine (his fashion label) khaki chinos with whales and skull and crossbones in Swarovski crystals all over, paired with basketball sneakers.

To enter Johnson's world is to immediately master the art of multitasking: your jaw drops as you try to take photos, catch his amazing source for the living room rug he found online for a song, ask him about the Spotify list he's playing, accept an espresso, and text Stacey who is still sleeping: "At Johnson's new place: RUN DON'T WALK!"

Johnson claims he has a long way to go to finish, but I can't see where: every surface has been wallpapered, many in various patterns from his already iconic first collection for Schumacher or painted in sunny yellows, clover greens, and in fat red, pink, and blue stripes (on the ceiling, no less) by the host himself. "When I moved in, we were in the middle of the pandemic," he explains. "I craved a sense of comfort."

Baskets dangle from the ceiling as you enter into the open kitchen and eating area, hence the new house's apt name: "Basket Case." It's a place that brims with crazy creativity, for sure, where Nantucket dioramas hang alongside Damien Hirst paintings and sixteenth-century continental oil portraits. It's all like being at some wonderful dinner party, where you may not remember what you ate the next morning but you retain every memorable conversation from the night before.

"I have new Libertine samples here; slip into something for our portrait," Johnson says, which is pretty much the best sentence a fashion designer can ever utter. He then hands me Libertine's Kandi Chintz blazer and matching shirt to wear. I recognize the pattern instantly from the curtains in the living room. Johnson often cross-pollinates Libertine fabrics in his houses.

Stacey usually can document me posing somewhere scenic alongside our host within minutes. But in Johnson's case, it takes almost an hour. First of all: How to choose the spot? Every nook here is more photogenic than the next. But it's not just the destination that's the problem; it's the visitor. In every shot, my mouth is open from laughing. Johnson's humor is both a blessing and a curse.

Before long, we're out of time, and poor Flower is squirming in her owner's arms, and it's still hard for me to keep a still expression. We show the portraits apologetically to Johnson and vow to take more. "There's no need," he says. "I like the imperfection. That's life."

··●●··

PREVIOUS SPREAD: The Grotto Room, where Johnson likes to host intimate lunches or breakfasts (and the occasional séance), is wallpapered in his Plates and Platters for Schumacher. He sponged-painted all trims, shutters, and the ceiling to give the nook a more unified look. "I've collected blue-and-white Chinese and English porcelain for a hundred years," says Johnson. "I've been waiting to have an entire B-and-W room for thirty years, and at some point every inch of wall space will be covered with real blue-and-white plates and platters over the wallpaper for a trippy illusionary experience."

OPPOSITE, TOP LEFT: "I've been in love with Brunschwig & Fils' Bibliotheque since I was a kid and finally found the perfect place to use it, in the under-stairs powder room," says Johnson.

OPPOSITE, TOP RIGHT: Flower, Johnson, and me wearing Libertine's Kandi Chintz.

OPPOSITE, BOTTOM: "I love creating outdoor vignettes to be seen from every window in the house," says Johnson. "I want them lush, verdant, and calming to look at."

In Basket Case's entry and living room, Johnson's goal was to create a deep sense of comfort and joy. "I put this house together during the worst pandemic in a hundred years, and wanted to use a little bit of everything I love. From hand-painted stripes on the ceiling of the foyer to one side of the front door painted green and the other pink, immediately when you enter, you're greeted by a wave of exuberance."

ABOVE: Vintage Christian Lacroix and coral necklaces on a junky bust of Caesar.

OPPOSITE: In the library, an eighteenth-century Irish Georgian mirror hangs above a sofa upholstered in Johnson's Jokhang Tiger fabric for Schumacher. Johnson found the camel in a thrift store, and it has become, along with Flower, the mascot of the house.

"Since I was a kid, I have loved the intimate miniature world of dioramas" says Johnson. "I've collected ship ones for over twenty years and have been told I have one of the largest collections in the world. I have nowhere near enough room for them all, so I rotate them in and out."

DESPITE
THE COST OF
LIVING
IT'S STILL
POPULAR

PREVIOUS SPREAD, LEFT: Johnson displays his antique Pashootan green-and-brown sponge-painted bowls (which inspired the sponge-painted staircase in the house) with English blue-and-white transfer ware over a nineteenth-century Irish cupboard. Johnson has collected the baskets that inspired the name of the house since he was a kid: "I had no idea how many I had until we started unpacking them. Necessity really is the mother of invention, as there was no place other than the ceiling for them to go!"

PREVIOUS SPREAD, RIGHT: In the main bathroom, Johnson wanted to re-create the exotic feeling inspired by some of the places he loves to travel to most—including India, Morocco, and Egypt. Moroccan green-and-white tile laid in a zigzag pattern sets the tone. With Iksel's Indian-inspired mural on one wall, and a Schumacher floral on the others, it's a pattern knock. Johnson commissioned his muralist Chris Evans to paint the mural on the door and faux tile around the doors. "It's nice to walk into the bathroom and feel like you're on holiday somewhere more exotic than Los Angeles," he says.

OPPOSITE: In his bedroom, walls are papered in Iksel's Italian Panoramic up to the crown molding. Johnson had Chris Evans paint the trees to continue onto the ceiling. "I wanted to feel as if I was sleeping in an old-growth Italian forest," he says. The 1974 painting behind the bed is by Duggie Fields, one of Johnson's favorite artists. The desk used as a bedside table is eighteenth-century Georgian.

FOLLOWING SPREAD: In the guest bedroom, Johnson's Modern Toile wallpaper for Schumacher and an Ikea duvet cover in black and white ensure his guests feel enveloped in whimsy, graphic appeal, and total comfort.

Acknowledgments

At Home with would simply not be possible without the invaluable support and talent of Stacey Bewkes, both behind and in front of the lens. This book is as much hers as it is mine.

And, of course, so much gratitude to the marvelous and equally invaluable Ellen Nidy, my Rizzoli editor, and Charles Miers, our fearless leader there.

And thank you, Kayleigh Jankowski, my always trusty and adept art director.

Finally, thank you to all of the hosts who opened their elegant doors and gave us the incredible honor of capturing their world for our *Quintessence* video series.

Photography Credits
All photographs by Stacey Bewkes with the exception of pages 128;
131 bottom right; 132-133; and 134, which are by Rachel Schwarz.

Endpapers
Plates & Platters wallpaper by Johnson Hartig/Libertine for
Schumacher, fschumacher.com

First published in the United States of America in 2022 by
Rizzoli International Publications, Inc.
300 Park Avenue South
New York, NY 10010
www.rizzoliusa.com

Publisher: Charles Miers
Editor: Ellen Nidy
Design: Kayleigh Jankowski
Production Manager: Alyn Evans
Managing Editor: Lynn Scrabis

Printed in China

2022 2023 2024 2025 2026 / 10 9 8 7 6 5 4 3 2 1

ISBN: 978-0-8478-7131-5
Library of Congress Control Number: 2021949160

Visit us online:
Facebook.com / RizzoliNewYork
instagram.com/rizzolibooks
twitter.com/Rizzoli_Books
pinterest.com/rizzolibooks
youtube.com/user/RizzoliNY
issuu.com/rizzoli